Cuban Writers on and off the Island

Contemporary Narrative Fiction

Twayne's World Authors Series

Latin American Literature

David William Foster, Editor
Arizona State University

TWAS 886

Cuban Writers on and off the Island

Contemporary Narrative Fiction

Pamela Maria Smorkaloff

New York University

Twayne Publishers
New York

#412 66105

Twayne's World Authors Series No. 886

Cuban Writers on and off the Island
Contemporary Narrative Fiction
Pamela Maria Smorkaloff

Twayne Publishers
1633 Broadway
New York, NY 10019

Library of Congress Cataloging-in-Publication Data

Smorkaloff, Pamela Maria, 1956–
     Cuban writers on and off the island : contemporary narrative
fiction / Pamela Maria Smorkaloff.
          p.   cm. — (Twayne's world authors series ; n. 886. Latin American
literature)
     Includes bibliographical references (p.   -   ) and index.
     ISBN 0-8057-1617-3 (alk. paper)
     1. Cuban fiction—20th century—History and criticism.   2. Cuban
fiction—Foreign countries—History and criticism.   I. Title.
II. Series: Twayne's world authors series ; TWAS 886.   III. Series:
Twayne's world authors series. Latin American literature.
PQ7382 .S66   1999
863—dc21   99-27604
                                                                            CIP

This paper meets the requirements of ANSI/NISO Z3948-1992 (Permanence of
Paper).

10 9 8 7 6 5 4 3 2

Printed in the United States of America

Contents

Preface   *ix*
Chronology   *xiii*

Chapter One
The Home and the World:
Situating the Twentieth-Century Cuban Literary Tradition   1

Chapter Two
Building the Cuban Canon: "Memories of the Future"   10

Chapter Three
Canon and Diaspora: A Literary Dialogue   27

Chapter Four
From Lost Steps to Hyphenated Lives:
Cuban Voices and Latino Literature   60

Conclusion   *75*
Notes and References   *83*
Selected Bibliography   *87*
Index   *97*

Preface

> I have noticed in contemporary Cuban literature a will toward integration with surrounding reality.
>
> —Jean-Michele Fossey

> That relationship with surrounding reality has always existed. It's a question of form.
>
> —José Lezama Lima, *Recopilación de textos sobre José Lezama Lima* (1970)

> The most Latin American novels of recent times have been written outside our borders.
>
> —Eduardo Galeano, in Claude Cymerman,
> "La literatura hispanoamericana en el exilio" (1988)

A decade ago, when the Cold War still cast its shadow over the academy, this study, had there been an audience for it, would have had a very different configuration. The history of Cuban literature, which I have been studying for the past two decades, has contained, from its very beginnings, writers who made their mark abroad, for any number of reasons, consolidated their fame at home, then left again, or never came back. Others never left the island while their oeuvre, their reputation as writers, traveled the globe.

Antonio Benítez Rojo brings into focus the global links made by the "Caribbean machine, whose flux, whose noise, whose presence covers the map of world history's contingencies."[1] Michael Dash, in his fine introduction to Édouard Glissant's *Caribbean Discourse,* observes that it is in "the untamed spectacle" of a Caribbean—indeed, an American landscape— that Glissant "locates the poetics of the cross-cultural imagination."[2] And the late Angel Rama defined the Caribbean as a zone in which "the plural manifestations of the entire universe insert themselves."[3]

The observations of these three writers, all American in the fullest sense, two from the Caribbean and one Latin American, pinpoint and summarize the diverse sources, flow, and spirit of contemporary Cuban literature to which this study pays tribute.

Cubans have historically written and produced an oeuvre both on and off the island. Many major literary figures have done both, working in

Havana and Madrid, Havana and Paris, Havana and New York or else-where, in a continuum and without contradiction. The majority of the diaspora writers studied have made their off-island homes and lives in the United States. Notable exceptions include Guillermo Cabrera Infante, whose work is not examined in depth in this study for reasons of thematic coherence. By virtue of taking London as his home base, Cab-rera Infante has abstracted himself from the Cold War polemic that has obsessively engaged the Cuban and U.S. publics for more than three decades. An undeniably important literary figure of our century, Cab-rera Infante has written of experiencing a complete rupture with the his-tory of the island, encountering a void where historical continuity had once been evident, upon his return from Brussels in 1965. I have chosen to concentrate on a corpus of writers of narrative fiction whose works exemplify a conscious engagement with the island's history as contin-uum, and therefore I have left the study of Cabrera Infante's works to other scholars, and other studies. The other notable exception to the rule of a Cuban diaspora based in the United States is Zoë Valdés, an important emerging novelist living in Paris, whose work, not yet pub-lished when I began writing, is discussed in the final chapter.

Until fairly recently, it was not uncommon to find approaches to con-temporary Cuban literature oriented along openly Cold War lines. One either studied the novel of the revolution or the novel of exile. Artifi-cially imposed lines of separation too often obscured the continuity of a literary tradition that lay behind points of rupture. Having wanted to challenge (and thus lend greater nuance to) the stark division of litera-ture into that of the revolution and that of exile, and because the greater part of the contemporary exiles and their offspring live in the United States, I have, of necessity, concentrated on twentieth-century Cuban-American literature. Omission of any contemporary off-island Cuban writers not residing in the United States responds to that logic, rather than any literary or aesthetic criteria.

Happily, the pendulum is swinging back once again within the United States, and there is currently a more complex, nuanced appreci-ation of both the sources that have fed twentieth-century Cuban litera-ture as well as the *cubanía* (Cubanness) of its creators. Since 1989 and the fall of the Berlin Wall, Cuban literature has been framed conceptu-ally in more flexible terms of canon and diaspora rather than the fixed spaces of revolution or exile. A growing awareness of the universality of the Caribbean through recent works by Glissant, Benítez Rojo, and oth-ers has certainly helped to reposition Cuban literature at this century's end. The movement of history over the course of the twentieth century to the present juncture, with momentous changes for Cuban society at either end, has brought Cuba once again into sharp focus. New voices have been emerging, in and outside of Cuba, and the classics are being revisited as a consequence of this "stretching" of the contemporary canon.

Edmundo Desnoes, in his 1981 anthology *Los dispositivos en la flor: Cuba, literatura desde la revolución,* boldly declared in his prologue: "No es un prólogo para cubanos" [This is not a prologue for Cubans], breaking with the old notion that a collection of Cuban narratives published in the United States would, whether welcomed or denounced, necessarily circulate primarily among Cuban-Americans. His, clearly, was a collection intended for outsiders to whom not everything would be self-evident.

Contemporary Cuban Writers on and off the Island will attempt to examine Cuban literature in its current expression, here and there, in keeping with the circumstances that usher in a new century for Cuba and the world. That is, to look at the Cuban literary tradition wherever it has emerged, set down roots, and grown, in a dialectic of rupture and continuity, fully recognizing the diverse forces that have and will continue to shape that tradition in the twenty-first century.

This study in no way strives to be definitive: it is only a beginning, an attempt to track trends in a literary tradition in flux, one that is branching out in untried directions, once again. As Cuba seeks new relations and new internal structures, Cuban and Cuban-American writers must situate themselves in a shifting landscape. There are no absolutes. Time-honored conceptual boundaries are breaking down; others are being drawn. The meanings of exile and revolution are not what they were, yet they still hold.

The spirit of this work goes against the grain of purists and purity and toward a messy, hybrid sense of culture as universal vocation. It lies, then, somewhere between the declarations of Willy Stokes, Enrique Cirule's informant for *Conversación con el último norteamericano,* a man who defines himself as "procesado en Estados Unidos y cubano por el tiempo" [processed in the United States and Cuban by virtue of time] and identified himself, in the 1970s, as the last living North American of the failed colony La Gloria, founded in Cuba in 1899, and David Rieff's informants in *The Exile: Cuba in the Heart of Miami,* who fear that the *cubanía* of the exile will be extinguished with their generation. Although it is true that their children and grandchildren cannot assume the identity of exiles from a country they have never seen, that does not mean they can sever, or have severed, all ties—collective, cultural, historical—with the island. They will be the ones to forge new links with the island, as many of the protagonists in works by Cuban-American writers such as Achy Obejas, Marisella Veiga, Virgil Suárez, and Cristina García, each with his or her own strategy and in his or her own voice, attempt to do. It falls to them, as well, and those who come after them, to determine where they stand in the shifting sands of late-twentieth-century Cuban-American life, as do the narrator in Oscar Hijuelos's *Our House in the Last World* and the collage of narrative voices in Roberto G. Fernández's *La vida es un special.* In this regard, contemporary Cuban-American fiction flows into the larger corpus of "hyphenated," "transplanted" writers, living and working outside of Latin America, more often than not in English, such as Dominican-American Julia Alvarez and Mexican-Americans Rolando Hinojosa and Sandra Cisneros, all of whom make up the more generalized Latino literary boom of the 1990s.

With regard to the Cubans and Cuban-Americans whose works this study will address, as forgers, heirs, and continuers of a long-standing literary tradition, the conceptual framework for analysis is, and must be, for now, admittedly speculative and theoretical. As Rubén Rumbaut has observed, the main protagonists of revolution and exile "are aging and passing on. They will pass into the collective memory of our history." Rumbaut anticipates, as I do, the dissolution of the "wall" dividing island and diaspora in the new century, and he asks: "What bridges will form then, and who will cross them?" He concludes that future generations may surprise us, since "theirs, after all, will be the last word."[4]

Acknowledgments

The encouragement, generosity, and assistance of many individuals and institutions have contributed to the development of this study; I cannot hope to acknowledge them all. My most sincere thanks to all of those mentioned as well as those I may have inadvertently left out.

To David William Foster, acquisitions editor for this work, for challenging me to take on a complex and difficult topic and encouraging me to see it through. His friendship and trust have been invaluable.

To Anne Davidson, Mark Zadrozny, and Margaret Dornfeld, my editors at Twayne, for their patience, understanding, and vision throughout the entire process.

To my colleagues and students at the Center for Latin American and Caribbean Studies of New York University for their warmth and camaraderie: Christopher Mitchell, Carmen Margarita Díaz, Sandy Lugo, Jake Miller, and Daniel Enríquez.

Special thanks to Rachel Wolcott, whose wonderful paper on Achy Obejas inspired and helped get me started.

To the many friends who read or listened to early versions of the study and enriched it with their own knowledge and scholarship on Cuba, the Caribbean, and the diaspora: Cynthia Oliver, Awilda Díaz, William Mills, and Harvey Neptune. With special gratitude to Orlando Hernández, an expert on Lezama Lima, for assistance with those pages devoted to the poet.

A los cubanos raros que me acompañan en todo. I owe a special debt of gratitude to the network of old and new Cuban friends and colleagues, here and there, for their integrity, intellectual independence, and critical insight. Our conversations over the course of many years have shaped my thought, opening the parts of it that were narrow or closed and sharpening the parts already open. Your collective influence began to shape this book before I knew I would write it; without you, it would not have been possible. To Eduardo Aparicio, Ernesto Pujol, and Osvaldo Monzón, pioneers in the visual arts, whose courageous oeuvre opens doors and transcends limits. To Danilo Figueredo and Dinorah Lima for sharing their published books and articles with me "hot off the press"; and to Judy Artime for letting me read her thesis and introducing me to the novels of Roberto G. Fernández. To Mirna Serrano, Dinorah Lima, and Manuela Schrier, for their fierce intelligence and loyal friendship. To Alberto Batista Reyes, who got me started on all of this.

To friend and colleague Mauricio Font, for making possible the Cuba Seminar Project of the CUNY Graduate Center in which I have been fruitfully involved for the last year and half, and for inviting me to host a panel on literature and the arts in Cuba in the 1990s. My special thanks to Miguel Barnet, for his oeuvre, his friendship, and for agreeing to be the commentator for that panel. His brilliant exposition helped clarify my own frame of analysis.

To Jane Gregory Rubin of the InterAmericas Society for her far-reaching vision and global embrace of the arts, in general, and for all that her spirited friendship has meant to me.

To friends and colleagues Diane Wachtell, André Schiffrin, Dawn Davis, Jerome Chou, and Jessica Blatt for their brilliant work and the space they have granted me within it.

To the memory of Haydée Vitali, friend and teacher, for everything that is truly important, always.

To Robin Andersen, who listened while I talked about the project, and ultimately helped me figure out how to structure it.

To Bill Hinchey, who listened critically, but not *too* critically, as I read fresh pages to him every evening.

Chronology: Selected Authors, Works, and Historical Events since 1900

1900–1909

1901   Novelist and essayist Renée Méndez Capote is born in Havana.

The Platt amendment, an amendment to the Cuban constitution, written and approved by the United States Congress and a convention of Cuban leaders, proclaims the right of the United States to intervene in Cuba at any time.

1902   The U.S. government hands political power over to Tomás Estrada Palma, and the Cuban Republic is inaugurated.

1903   Miguel del Carrión (b. Havana, 1875) publishes *El milagro* (novel) (Havana: Tipografía particular de Azul y Rojo) and *La última voluntad. El doctor Riso. En familia. De la guerra. Inocencia* (stories) (Havana: Alberto Castillo).

1904   Novelist, short story writer, and essayist Alejo Carpentier is born in Havana.

1905   Fernando Ortiz (b. Havana, 1881) publishes his first major study, *Las simpatías de Italia por los mambises cubanos: Documentos para la historia de la independencia de Cuba,* in Marseilles.

1910–1919

1910   José Lezama Lima, poet, novelist, and founder of the Orígenes movement and journal, is born in Havana.

1915   Sugar prices rise, and the inflationary period known as the "Dance of Millions" begins. Cuban currency circulates on the island for the first time.

1917   Miguel del Carrión, *Las honradas* (novel) (Havana: Librería Nueva).

1918   Miguel del Carrión, *Las impuras* (novel) (Havana: Librería Nueva).

1920–1929

1920   José Rodríguez Feo, a prominent cultural figure, essayist, and translator, coeditor of the journal *Orígenes* (1944–1956) and founder of the journal *Ciclón* (1955–1957), is born in Havana.

1921   Novelist and essayist Antonio Benítez Rojo is born in Havana.

1927   The Grupo Minorista, a group of young Cuban writers and intellectuals led by Rubén Martínez Villena, is officially formed to combat government corruption and work toward cultural and political reform.

1929   Communist leader Julio Antonio Mella is assassinated by Cuban police agents in Mexico, and President Gerardo Machado begins his second term in office.

Novelist, short story writer, and essayist Guillermo Cabrera Infante is born in Gibara.

1930–1939

1930   Student protests against Machado increase. Constitutional guarantees are suspended, and the University of Havana is shut down.

Novelist and essayist Edmundo Desnoes is born in Havana.

Poet and novelist Pablo Armando Fernández is born in Central Delicias, Oriente.

Poet, essayist, and literary critic Roberto Fernández Retamar is born in Havana.

1933   Gerardo Machado is forced to step down and flees with his family to Nassau. Carlos Manuel de Céspedes is appointed president with the support of the United States.

Alejo Carpentier, *¡Écue-Yamba-Ó!: Historia afrocubana* (novel) (Madrid: Editorial España).

1937   José Lezama Lima, *Muerte de Narciso* (poetry) (Havana: Úcar, García).

1938   José Lezama Lima, *Coloquio con Juan Ramón Jiménez* (essay) (Havana: Publicaciones de la Secretaría de Educación).

1940–1949

1940   Novelist, poet, and ethnographer Miguel Barnet is born in Havana.

Fernando Ortiz, *Contrapunteo cubano del tabaco y el azúcar* (essay) (Havana: Jesús Montero, 1940).

1941   Novelist, short story writer, and essayist Jesús Díaz is born in Havana.

José Lezama Lima, *Enemigo rumor* (poetry) (Havana: Úcar, García).

1943   Novelist Reinaldo Arenas is born in Holguín, Oriente.

1944   José Lezama Lima and José Rodríguez Feo found the Orígenes group and the journal *Orígenes* (1944–1956). Members of the group also include the writers Gastón Baquero, Eliseo Diego, Samuel Feijóo, Pablo Armando Fernández, Fina García Marrus, Lorenzo García, Angel Gaztelú, Fayad Jamís, Luis Marré, Pedro de Oráa, Virgilio Piñera, Justo Rodríguez Santo, and Octavio Smith. They also jointly found a literary press, Ediciones Orígenes, which publishes works by the group's members.

Alejo Carpentier, *Viaje a la semilla* (novella) (Havana: Úcar, García).

1945   José Lezama Lima, *Aventuras sigilosas* (poetry) (Havana: Ediciones Orígenes).

1946   Alejo Carpentier, *La música en Cuba* (essays) (Mexico: Fondo de Cultura Económica).

1949   Alejo Carpentier, *El reino de este mundo* (novel) (Mexico: Edición y Distribución Iberoamericana de Publicaciones), and *Tristán e Isolda en Tierra Firme* (essays) (Caracas: Imprenta Nacional).

José Lezama Lima, *La fijeza* (poetry) (Havana: Ediciones Orígenes).

Essayist, poet, and literary critic Gustavo Pérez Firmat is born in Havana.

1950–1959

1950   José Lezama Lima, *Arístides Fernández* (essays) (Havana: Dirección de Cultura del Ministerio de Educación).

1951   Novelist and short story writer Roberto G. Fernández is born in Sagua la Grande.

Novelist Oscar Hijuelos is born in New York.

1952   Edmundo Desnoes, *Todo está en juego* (stories and poetry) (Havana: Ediciones Nosotros).

Fulgencio Batista leads a successful coup d'état against President Prío, who leaves the country.

1953   José Lezama Lima, *Analecta del reloj* (essays) (Havana: Ediciones Orígenes).

Alejo Carpentier, *Los pasos perdidos* (novel) (Mexico: Edición y Distribución Iberoamericana de Publicaciones).

Pablo Armando Fernández, *Salterio y lamentaciones (1951–1953)* (poetry) (Havana: Úcar, García).

Fidel Castro, leader of the younger members of the Orthodox Party, organizes for the overthrow of the Batista regime. Castro and a group of rebels seize the Moncada garrison in Santiago de Cuba, take control of a nearby radio station, and appeal to the people to rise up against Batista. The garrison is retaken by the army, many of the rebels are tortured and killed, and Castro is taken alive to a civil jail.

1955   Pablo Armando Fernández, *Nuevos poemas* (poetry) (New York: Las Américas).

1956   Novelist, short story writer, and journalist Achy Obejas is born in Havana.

Organized resistance to Batista by guerrilla forces of the rebel army begins in the Sierra Maestra Mountains.

Alejo Carpentier, *El acoso* (novel) (Buenos Aires: Editorial Losada), and *Guerra del tiempo* (three stories and a novel) (Mexico: Compañía General de Ediciones).

1957   José Lezama Lima, *La expresión americana* (essays) (Havana: Ministerio de Educación, Instituto Nacional de Cultura).

Short story writer Marisella Veiga is born in Havana and emigrates to the United States with her family in 1960.

1958   José Lezama Lima, *Tratados en La Habana* (essays) (Havana: Universidad Central de las Villas).

Novelist Cristina García is born in Havana.

1959   Poet and novelist Zoë Valdés is born in Havana.

On January 9, the rebel army enters Havana, victorious, with Fidel Castro at the head of its columns.

The Casa de las Américas literary and cultural center is founded, and the literary contest, which was to launch numerous Latin American and Caribbean writers, is established. The following year, in 1960, Casa begins publishing a literary journal, the prestigious *Revista Casa de las Américas,* and acquires its own publishing house to print the works of award-winning authors.

1960–1969

1960   José Lezama Lima, *Dador* (poetry) (Havana: Úcar, García).

Guillermo Cabrera Infante, *Así en la paz como en la guerra* (short stories) (Havana: Ediciones R).

In April, the Bay of Pigs invasion takes place, known in Cuba as "Playa Girón."

1961   Edmundo Desnoes, *No hay problema* (novel) (Havana: Ediciones R).

Pablo Armando Fernández, *Toda la poesía* (poetry) (Havana: Ediciones R).

The United States severs diplomatic relations with Cuba.

1962   Alejo Carpentier, *El siglo de las luces* (novel) (Mexico: Compañía General de Ediciones).

Pablo Armando Fernández, *Himnos* (poetry) (Havana: Librería La Tertulia).

The Cuban Missile Crisis arises and is resolved diplomatically. The United States imposes a full trade embargo against Cuba.

The Unión Nacional de Escritores y Artistas de Cuba (National Union of Cuban Writers and Artists) is founded.

Novelist and short story writer Virgil Suárez is born in Cuba and emigrates to the United States in the 1970s.

1963   Miguel Barnet, *La piedrafina y el pavorreal* (poetry) (Havana: Ediciones Unión).

Renée Méndez Capote, *Memorias de una cubanita que nació con el siglo* (novel) (Havana: Universidad Central de las Villas).

Edmundo Desnoes, *El cataclismo* (novel) (Havana: Ediciones R).

1964   Miguel Barnet, *Isla de güijes* (poetry) (Havana: Ediciones El Puente).

Alejo Carpentier, *Tientos y diferencias* (essays) (Mexico: Universidad Autónoma).

Pablo Armando Fernández, *El libro de los héroes* (poetry) (Havana: Casa de las Américas).

1965   Cabrera Infante severs his relations with the revolutionary government and with Cuba. He emigrates to England the following year.

Edmundo Desnoes, *Memorias del subdesarrollo* (novel) (Havana: Ediciones Unión).

1966   Miguel Barnet, *Biografía de un cimarrón* (testimonial novel) (Havana: Instituto de Etnología y Folklore).

Jesús Díaz, *Los años duros* (stories) (Havana: Casa de las Américas).

1967   Reinaldo Arenas, *Celestino antes del alba* (novel) (Havana: Ediciones Unión).

Guillermo Cabrera Infante, *Tres tristes tigres* (novel) (Barcelona: Seix Barral).

Miguel Barnet, *La sagrada familia* (poetry) (Havana: Casa de las Américas).

Antonio Benítez Rojo, *Tute de reyes* (stories) (Havana: Casa de las Américas). The work wins the 1967 Casa prize.

Edmundo Desnoes, *Punto de vista* (essays) (Havana: Instituto del Libro).

1969   Reinaldo Arenas, *El mundo aluncinante: Una novela de aventuras* (novel) (Mexico: Editorial Diógenes).

Miguel Barnet, *La canción de Rachel* (testimonial novel) (Havana: Instituto del Libro).

Antonio Benítez Rojo, *El escudo de hojas secas* (stories) (Havana: Ediciones Unión).

1970–1979

1970   Pablo Armando Fernández, *Los niños se despiden* (novel) (Havana: Casa de las Américas), and *Un sitio permanente* (poetry) (Madrid: Ediciones Rialp).

José Lezama Lima, *La cantidad hechizada* (essays) (Havana: UNEAC).

Alejo Carpentier, *Literatura y conciencia política en América Latina* and *La ciudad de las columnas* (essays) (Barcelona: Editorial Lumen).

1971   The Padilla affair occurs, following the publication of *Fuera de juego,* a volume of poems by Heberto Padilla that caused a scandal inside of Cuba, made him a cause célèbre outside of Cuba, and was believed by many to have launched Casa de las América's more militant phase of Pan-American cultural activism.

The first Congreso de Educación y Cultura (Congress on Education and Culture) is held in Havana, with delegates from all the ministries and major cultural institutions nationwide in attendance.

Roberto Fernández Retamar, *Calibán: Apuntes sobre la cultura en nuestra América* (essays) (Mexico: Editorial Diógenes).

1972   Alejo Carpentier, *El derecho de asilo* (novella) (Barcelona: Editorial Lumen).

1974   Alejo Carpentier, *Concierto barroco* and *El recurso del método* (novels) (Mexico: Siglo Veintiuno).

Guillermo Cabrera Infante, *Vista del amanecer en el trópico* (novel) (Barcelona: Seix Barral).

1975   Roberto G. Fernández, *Cuentos sin rumbo* (stories) (Miami: Ediciones Universal).

1976   The Ministry of Culture is created, inaugurating a new and more coherent phase in Cuban cultural policy.

José Lezama Lima dies in Havana.

Guillermo Cabrera Infante, *Exorcismos de esti(l)o* (stories) (Madrid: Seix Barral).

1978   Alejo Carpentier, *Consagración de la primavera* (novel) (Mexico: Siglo Veintiuno).

Miguel Barnet, *Akeke y la jutía* (Cuban tales) (Havana: UNEAC).

1979   Guillermo Cabrera Infante, *La Habana para un infante difunto* (novel) (Madrid: Seix Barral).

Alejo Carpentier, *El arpa y la sombra* (novel) (Mexico: Siglo Veintiuno).

Antonio Benítez Rojo, *El mar de las lentejas* (novel) (Havana: Letras Cubanas).

1980–1989

1980   After a small group occupies the Peruvian Embassy in Havana, the government permits more than 100,000 Cubans seeking asylum to begin a chaotic exodus to the United States through a boat lift out of Mariel harbor, during the Carter presidency.

Miguel Barnet, *Orikis y otros poemas* (poetry) (Havana: Letras Cubanas).

Reinaldo Arenas flees Cuba, taking up residence in New York, as part of the Mariel boat lift.

Alejo Carpentier dies in Havana.

1981   Roberto G. Fernández, *La vida es un special, .75* (novel) (Miami: Ediciones Universal).

Reinaldo Arenas, *Termina el desfile* (novel) (Barcelona: Seix Barral).

1982   Reinaldo Arenas, *Cantando en el pozo* and *Otra vez el mar* (novels) (Barcelona: Argos Vergara).

Miguel Barnet, *Carta de noche* (poetry) (Havana: Letras Cubanas).

1983   Reinaldo Arenas, *El palacio de las blanquísimas mofetas* (novel) (Barcelona: Argos Vergara).

Miguel Barnet, *Gallego* (testimonial novel) and *La fuente viva* (essays) (Havana: Letras Cubanas).

Oscar Hijuelos, *Our House in the Last World* (novel) (New York: Persea).

1984   Reinaldo Arenas, *Arturo, la estrella más brillante* (novel) (Barcelona: Montesinos).

Miguel Barnet and Angel L. Fernández, eds., *Ensayos etnográficos/Fernando Ortiz* (essays) (Havana: Editorial de Ciencias Sociales).

Miguel Barnet, *La vida real* (testimonial novel) (Madrid: Ediciones Alfaguara).

1985   Roberto G. Fernández, *La montaña rusa* (novel) (Houston: Arte Público).

Guillermo Cabrera Infante, *Holy Smoke* (novel) (New York: Harper and Row). The novel was originally written in English.

1987   Jesús Díaz, *Las iniciales de la tierra* (novel) (Havana: Letras Cubanas). Following Carpentier's *Consagración de la primavera,* Díaz's is the second major novel to take as its central theme the revolutionary process in Cuba.

Reinaldo Arenas, *La loma del ángel* (novel) (Malaga: Dador Ediciones).

Miguel Barnet, *Viendo mi vida pasar* (poetry) (Havana: Letras Cubanas).

1988   Roberto G. Fernández, *Raining Backwards* (novel) (Houston: Arte Público). Fernández's novel and Oscar Hijuelos's *Our House in the Last World* are among the first Cuban-American novels to be written in English and published in the United States.

Enrique Cirules, *Conversación con el último norteamericano* (testimonial novel) (Havana: Letras Cubanas).

1989   The Berlin Wall comes down, leading ultimately to the collapse of the eastern socialist bloc nations; Cuba loses its trading partners and enters a prolonged crisis that came to be known as the "Special Period."

Antonio Benítez Rojo, *La isla que se repite: El Caribe y la perspectiva posmoderna* (essays) (Hanover: Ediciones del Norte).

Miguel Barnet, *Oficio de Angel* (novel) (Madrid: Alfaguara).

Pablo Armando Fernández, *El vientre del pez* (novel) (Havana: Letras Cubanas).

1990–1999

1990   Reinaldo Arenas, after battling AIDS, commits suicide in New York.

Julio Girona, *Seis horas y más* (testimonial novel) (Havana: Letras Cubanas).

Oscar Hijuelos, *The Mambo Kings Play Songs of Love* (novel) (New York: Perennial Library).

1991   Virgil Suárez, *The Cutter* (novel) (New York: Ballantine).

1992   Guillermo Cabrera Infante, *Mea Cuba* (essays) (Barcelona: Plaza y Janés, Cambio 16).

Cristina García, *Dreaming in Cuban* (novel) (New York: Knopf).

Virgil Suárez, *Welcome to the Oasis and Other Stories* (stories) (Houston: Arte Público).

Virgil Suárez and Delia Poey, eds., *Iguana Dreams: New Latino Fiction* (prose fiction) (New York: HarperPerennial).

1993   Oscar Hijuelos, *The Fourteen Sisters of Emilio Móntez O'Brien* (novel) (New York: Farrar, Straus and Giroux).

Zoë Valdés, *Sangre azul* (novel) (Havana: Letras Cubanas).

1994   Achy Obejas, *We Came All the Way from Cuba So You Could Dress like This?* (stories) (San Francisco: Cleis Press).

1995   An encounter between Cuban writers and exiled Cuban writers, representing the older generation, is held in Switzerland.

Miguel Barnet, *Cultos afrocubanos: La Regla de Ocha, la Regla de Palo Monte* (essays) (Havana: Ediciones Unión).

Roberto G. Fernández, *Holy Radishes!* (novel) (Houston: Arte Público).

Oscar Hijuelos, *Mr. Ives' Christmas* (novel) (New York: Harper Collins).

Gustavo Pérez Firmat, *Next Year in Cuba: A Cubano's Coming-of-Age in America* (memoir) (New York: Anchor Books).

Virgil Suárez, *Havana Thursdays* (novel) (Houston: Arte Público).

Zoë Valdés, *La nada cotidiana* (novel) (Barcelona: Emecé Editores), and *La hija del embajador* (novel) (Baleares: Bitzoc).

1996 A group of Cuban-American writers, including Achy Obejas, Cristina García, and others representing the younger generation, are invited to Havana for a literary exchange with their contemporaries on the island.

Guillermo Cabrera Infante, *Delito por bailiar el chachachá* (stories) (Madrid: Santillana).

Alejo Carpentier, *El amor a la ciudad* (journalistic writings) (Madrid: Alfaguara).

Jesús Díaz, *La piel y la máscara* (novel) (Barcelona: Editorial Anagrama). Written in exile, in Berlin.

Achy Obejas, *Memory Mambo* (novel) (San Francisco: Cleis Press).

Virgil Suárez, *Going Under* (novel) (Houston: Arte Público).

Zoë Valdés, *Cólera de ángeles* (novel) (Barcelona: Textuel), and *Te di la vida entera* (novel) (Barcelona: Planeta).

1997 Zoë Valdés, *Café nostalgia* (novel) (Barcelona: Planeta).

Cristina García, *The Agüero Sisters* (novel) (New York: Knopf).

1998 In January, Pope John Paul II makes a historic visit to Cuba.

The New Yorker publishes a special issue on Cuba (January 26), with "Miosvatis," a short story by Miguel Barnet, as the central fiction piece.

Chapter One

The Home and the World: Situating the Twentieth-Century Cuban Literary Tradition

> Not caring to conquer, but playing the game of the world . . . porous to all the breath of the world.
>
> —Aimé Césaire, *Cahier d'un retour au pays natal* (1947)

Scholars have worked long and hard to define the elements that make up the Cuban literary tradition of our century. The result has been a steady outpouring of critical reflections on Cuban literature, often by the writers themselves, charting it at every stage of its development. Across the decades, on and off the island, literary studies have been as prolific as the literary production on which they reflect. The aim of this chapter is not to reiterate but rather to point to that body of work as a map, a historical bridge to those writers just now emerging or those whose works are being revisited today. One of the constants of the Cuban literary tradition, of both canon and diaspora, has been the tension between the "home" and the "world," between the regional and the universal, in the construction of identity within the context of nation and national culture. The problem is that "home" is never a static entity or space but one propelled and shaped by conflict, projected onto history's arena. The "world," in turn, is constantly being redrawn. Ramón Gutiérrez and Genaro Padilla suggest, in the introduction to their edited volume *Recovering the U.S. Hispanic Literary Heritage,* that categories overlap "when the author lives a transnational reality," and that they may, in any case, be irrelevant in the context of Cuban literature and Cuban-American literature because there are no easy answers to the question "where does one end and the other begin?"[1]

It is perhaps only by situating Cuban literature on the time line of twentieth-century history that we can begin to understand the narrative universe of the most contemporary of Cuban-American writers. If the

now classic Alejo Carpentier and the new, off-island novelist Achy Obejas serve as markers of a kind of transnational literary map, one can
move between the works of major literary figures, those who shaped the
canon and those writing now, to establish a dynamic, a new literary dialogue.

The events of the last fin de siècle, of 1898, and their impact were
not immediately reflected in the Cuban literary imagination. At first,
there was relative silence among Cuban writers. It would take more
than a decade, until the 1920s, for the effects of the momentous shift,
the "mortal leap" into the twentieth century and the disillusionment it
brought, to find expression in national literature, with the notable
exception of Miguel de Carrión's *Las honradas* and *Las impuras* of 1918
and 1919, respectively. Similarly, the events of, and those leading up to,
1959 and the Cuban revolution have been simmering, taking form in
literature in fits and starts, over time. Prose fiction of the 1960s and
1970s tended to be largely retrospective in its gaze, an exploration of
the past from a newly gained perspective. Carpentier's *Consagración de la
primavera* (1978)—which has yet to be translated into English—and
Jesús Díaz's *La iniciales de la tierra* (1987), novels generally held to take
the 1959 revolution as their point of departure, theme, and even protagonist, incubated for several decades before the writing was undertaken.

Stated in the most general terms, contemporary Cuban-American
narratives claim the same historical moment as impulse and point of
departure. They have, until recently, been of a markedly nostalgic and
evocative tone, with identity—Cuban identity—as dream: that is, a
part of consciousness preserved yet on hold; a realm to be evoked, not
confronted in active engagement.

The distance, and the tension, between home and world are measured in the journey from one to the other. I take Achy Obejas's writing,
very much of the 1990s in which it emerged, as a marker of a spectrum,
like the canonical master Carpentier, because her work takes on Cuban-
Americanness, exploring actively and rigorously what it means to be
Cuban-American in the United States today in much the same way that
Carpentier's characters have shaped, from the 1930s to the present,
questions of Cubanness in the collective consciousness. It is no coinci-
dence that both Carpentier and Obejas have as their primary experience
that of coming of age in a land distinct from that of their parents, Carpentier as a child of immigrants and Obejas as a child immigrant. For
both, raising the right questions and looking for answers entails journey.

No matter how many displacements, the journey always leads back to Cuba.

It is intergenerational conflict, centered on vision, memory, and the interpretation of memory, that propels a writer such as Achy Obejas *to* Cuba, back to the Caribbean, to sort things out. For Obejas, like Carpentier, displacement, voluntary or otherwise, is a journey that leads the protagonists alternately away from or toward consciousness. Carpentier's self-consciously titled novella "Journey Back to the Source" ("Viaje a la semilla," 1944) chronicles a process in reverse, that of peeling off the layers of false consciousness that went into the making of the nineteenth-century Creole aristocracy of Havana. Only by shedding all the layers and attaining a kind of degree zero of consciousness can the Marquis begin again, return to the source, question identity from a position of clarity. For Obejas's Cuban-American characters, exile is false memory, or rather a fixed set of false memories that constitute a dangerous and ultimately destructive mirage. The reader cannot help but root for the protagonists who consciously set out to clear a path out of the mirage and into historical consciousness as the community acts in concert to weave the web of false memory tighter around the transgressor, excluding all but the mutually agreed on version. In her debut collection's title story "We Came All the Way from Cuba So You Could Dress like This?" the nameless female first-person narrator cuts back and forth in time across the significant events in the shaping of her consciousness, beginning with her arrival from Cuba with her parents, at age 10. Her homecoming from college in Indiana in 1971 marks the distance she has traveled from the fuzzy, insulated memory of the group to a clarity all her own. For her parents and their generation, surface and center, memory and image, must be all of a piece, distorted in equal measure to allow for no apparent contradictions. The bell-bottomed blue jeans she wears, together with the air of the antiwar demonstrations she has just come from, shatter the coherence the parents have striven to forge and hold together: "We left Cuba so you could dress like this? my father will ask over my mother's shoulder. . . . And for the first and only time in my life, I'll say, Look, you didn't come for me, you came for you; you came because all your rich clients were leaving, and you were going to wind up a cashier in your father's hardware store if you didn't leave, okay?"[2]

Unlike her parents, the narrator's consciousness is integral, independent, sharp, and true to itself throughout, registering both the said and the unsaid, the remembered and the unremembered of others' selective

recall, with uncompromising honesty. This, the first, clearing of the air
or settling of accounts sets up a chain of associations in the narrator's
memory that charts the successive juxtapositions of official and unofficial versions of events in the family mythology, under the heading of
"things that can't be told": "Like knowing that giving money to exile
groups often meant helping somebody buy a private yacht for
Caribbean vacations, not for invading Cuba, but also knowing that
refusing to donate only invited questions about our own patriotism. . . .
And knowing that Nixon really wasn't the one, and wasn't doing anything, and wouldn't have done anything, even if he'd finished his second
term, no matter what a good job the Cuban burglars might have done
at the Watergate Hotel" (*We Came,* 124).

Which, in turn, pushes the narrator's consciousness, her historical
imagination, personal and collective, back toward Cuba, across the span
of the years she was absent, though she was too young to have chosen
that absence, and a rich, logical string of what-ifs: "What if we'd
stayed? What if we'd never left Cuba? What if we were there when the
last of the counterrevolution was beaten, or when Mariel harbor leaked
thousands of Cubans out of the island, or when the Pan-American
Games came? What if we'd never left ?" (*We Came,* 124).

Her consciousness continually returns to the moment of arrival in
Miami, to scenes from the INS processing center and the nights spent
in the transient hotel, paid for with taxpayer dollars. For the parents,
arrival in Miami marks the end of the journey. They will convince
themselves of that, through the strategy of false memory, spinning out
as many versions as necessary to reinforce the static truth that *this* is
their ultimate destination, no matter how many doubts they have
pushed back along the way. In contrast, the narrator's consciousness
spreads out in the opposite direction, away from the confines of exile
and toward the untamed world, cultivating doubt and impassioned
skepticism. Her mind returns to the port, Miami, as point of orientation and point of departure. Where her parents' journey ends, hers
begins: "And as I lie here wondering about the spectacle outside the
window and the new world that awaits us on this and every night of
the rest of our lives, even I know we've already come a long way. What
none of us can measure yet is how much of the voyage is already behind
us" (*We Came,* 131).

Obejas's sharp young narrator and her parents have widely divergent
appreciations of surrounding reality, and radically different responses to
the existential questions of who they are, where they have come from,

and where they are going. At the story's conclusion, the young girl anticipates, with a certain joy and without hesitation, the risks that change implies, the possibility of exploring and engaging with the "new world" beyond the hotel window, whatever it may hold.

On a symbolic level, no barriers hold the narrator back from the active engagement she seeks with reality. She is thus, and will continue to be, a reliable witness to, and narrator of, events precisely because she is an active participant. The parents, on the other hand, hold off on buying a new television set, not because they don't want one, but because (as the father repeats daily) they will be going "home" at any moment. When they do relent and buy a television, it is for watching boxing and other sports, a window to little else. This chasm between the characters defines the contours and reveals the sources of a generational divide that deepens and grows into a total breakdown of communication, and ultimately violence. The father's immobility, his spiritual and historical stasis, causes him to paralyze temporarily the daughter, literally knocking her down with kicks and blows, since he cannot otherwise prevent her from growing away from him and into the world around her. His rage stems, in large part, less from his daughter's attitude than from the realization that he cannot prevent himself from becoming historically irrelevant. This is important not only for the story's denouement, highlighting the daughter's liberation and the parents' stagnation, but for identifying two substantive strains in contemporary Cuban literature: active engagement, movement, journey, a universalist vocation, on the one hand, and nostalgia, on the other. Consciousness moves in two substantive directions, seeking either engagement with or evasion from sociohistorical reality. Both are evident in contemporary Cuban literature.

Carpentier's *The Kingdom of This World* (*El reino de este mundo*, 1949) gave us his theory of *lo real maravilloso* (the marvelous-real), defined in the prologue that introduces the work. In preparing to write a novel set in Haiti before, during, and immediately after the revolution that began in 1791, Carpentier set himself the writer's task of exploring the intersection of the historical and literary imaginations in the so-called New World, the meanings and uses of myth, syncretism, faith, and the relationship of past, present, and future in the consciousness of a community. The result of these reflections is his theory of *lo real maravilloso* in American literature, which is ultimately much more an immersion in the historical making of the Americas than a rejection of the European-style surrealism to which he had been exposed, though it is that too.

Carpentier explains its essence as follows: "[B]ecause of the dramatic singularity of the events, because of the fantastic bearing of the characters who met, at a given moment, in the magical crossroads of Cap-Haitien, everything seems marvelous in a story it would have been impossible to set in Europe and which is as real, in any case, as any exemplary event yet set down for the edification of students in school manuals. But what is the history of all the Americas but a chronicle of the real marvelous?"[3]

His subsequent novel, *The Lost Steps* (*Los pasos perdidos,* 1953), which will be discussed in detail in the next chapter, is structured on a double axis that explores both historical layering and sources of cultural identity in the Americas, as well as the violence implicit in the juxtaposition of "old" and "new" worlds understood not as a closed chapter of the historical past but as an ongoing process. Written as chronicle, as the travel diary of a nameless protagonist's journey from New York to the heart of Latin America, the other America of his birth and childhood, the novel may—and I believe should—also be read as a theory of Latin American culture. In the protagonist's missteps, in all that he misses along the way to a failed self-discovery, all the paths not taken, the reader finds an invaluable guide for seeking out the sources that have and continue to shape cultural identity in Latin America. Carpentier's "cross-cultural imagination" invariably moves, as do the trajectories of most of his novels, back and forth across an axis that connects Europe and America, America and Europe. Here and there, then and now, are for Carpentier connected in essential, inevitable ways, so that exploring Europe is one of the many ways to explore Latin America, as he does in *Explosion in a Cathedral* (*El siglo de las luces,* 1962). All three novels examine societal upheaval at a crucial moment in history, pausing to study, with great attention to detail, the moment before change erupts, whether in Haiti, Venezuela, or Spain. The novelist repeatedly casts his gaze across the fresco of history, taking in all that leads up to the moment when a society overturns its own hierarchy. Through these multiple, global points of reference, he gains a better grasp of the protracted process of upheaval in his own society, which he will focus on more directly in one of his last novels, *Consagración de la primavera,* 1978.

To put it another way (as Cuban novelist, poet, and social anthropologist Miguel Barnet did recently on a panel we shared on the subject of contemporary Cuban arts and letters), all Cubans, wherever they are, hold a common obsession with 1959. For all, inescapably and without exception, that year stands as a defining moment. It colors, shapes, and informs both self-perception and perception of the world, context, the individual's relationship to historical process, national and international, and how he or she views the island's articulation with the world. January 1959 marks for some the moment when the island closed in on itself. For others, it signaled Cuba's projection into history in its own right, a full opening to the crosscurrents of the world. Either way, it is an inescapable historical and existential fact. To return once more to Desnoes's prologue to *Los dispositivos en la flor,* it was to be an anthology of contemporary Cuban writing that he hoped would, as an ensemble, "allow us to see, to recognize, the complexity, the intensity of a revolutionary process from which none of the inhabitants of Cuba can abstract themselves. Not even in exile."[4]

Fueled by the Cold War, which touched the lives of Cubans on and off the island, the historical debate over what it meant to be Cuban acquired a white-hot urgency when it came to revolve exclusively around the 1959 revolution. That year produced a new exile, one that North Americanized the terms of the debate, reducing the universal range of Cubanness to the two poles of Havana and Miami. Certainly, within the United States, people began to lose sight of the ongoing existence of a Cuban diaspora, one that spread across Europe, Latin America, and the United States, too. They seemed also to forget that the nation's most prized writers—from Esteban Borrero and his daughter Juana in the early 1800s to Cirilo Villaverde and José Martí toward the close of the last century—had lived, written, and published off the island, long before the tensions of the 1950s erupted. Eclipsed from memory as well, by the obsession with 1959, are all those who went into exile in the 1930s, among them anthropologist Fernando Ortiz, whose *Cuban Counterpoint,* long out of print in English, has just been reissued by Duke University Press. Ortiz went into exile in the United States in 1931 and stayed for four years, teaching and militating against Machado and the U.S. influence in Cuba, before he returned for good.

That none of these earlier displaced writers ever became "hyphenated" is an important distinction. Hyphenated writers, whatever their orientation may be, live and create on a permanent axis that connects their ties to their country of origin with their daily American lives. That is the case of the Cuban-American and other hyphenated writers who will be studied in chapters 3 and 4, relating contemporary Cuban-American writing to the Cuban canon, and to the larger Latino literary boom. In its entirety, this study sets out to trace the arc that stretches from the founders of the twentieth-century tradition of Cuban narrative to a representative group of very contemporary Cuban-American writers who spring from the canon and enrich it dialectically, with the twist of a new landscape, a new language, and a critical distance often absent in earlier Cuban-American fiction.

When asked why her novel *How the García Girls Lost Their Accents* moves backward in time, Dominican-American writer Julia Alvarez responds succinctly: "Because that is how memory functions." This inverse movement, she adds, "is peculiar to those who abandon their country. You run a risk: that of falling into the constant nostalgia of idealizing the past. Like constructing a Garden of Eden in the territory of Memory. In my case that would be to imagine an idyllic childhood on that island when in truth there was an abominable dictatorship, with disappeared and terror."[5]

Alvarez describes the hyphen of her writer's existence as a space of conflict, rather than complacency or nostalgia. The hyphen sparked her writer's imagination precisely because it is "the place where two worlds collide."[6]

Memory, competing visions and versions of events in the narration of a nation, and the tensions between home and world inform all Cuban literature of this century. But the off-island production of contemporary Cuban-American writers, in addition to such tensions, is much more weighted by memory, and the challenge of finding narrative strategies for engaging with the past without falling into the trap of idealizing it.

I have taken the concepts of the home and the world as context, as a framework for exploring the contemporary Cuban literary tradition in an inclusive sense, to acknowledge the blurring of boundaries and the fragility of borders. The journey is often a structuring motif in modern Cuban literature, whether it is a journey within the self, the home, and the family, as in José Lezama Lima's *Paradiso,* or a journey that spans centuries and continents, as in Alejo Carpentier's *El siglo de las luces.* Yet the journey is inevitably triggered in the literary imagination by the tensions between the regional and the universal, the home and the world, the individual and the community, be it the family or the nation-state. In all of this, in Cuban as in all Caribbean and Latin American literature, there is a reaction against the Europe that placed itself in the role of owner and keeper of culture. The journey, then, serves as a means of escape from the binding stamp of "insularity" imposed on the islands by Europe and a movement back to the universality of the Caribbean as crossroads, as generator of a cross-cultural aesthetic.

The next chapter, "Building the Cuban Canon: 'Memories of the Future,' " examines the works of major Cuban narrators, those who formed the twentieth-century canon. Some, such as José Lezama Lima, Edmundo Desnoes, and Renée Méndez Capote, remained at home in their narratives; some did not, such as Alejo Carpentier, Miguel Barnet, and Pablo Armando Fernández, among others whose successive displacements lent a particular structure and rhythm to their prose creations. Figures such as Reinaldo Arenas, whose career was launched in Cuba and continued to develop off the island, in a permanent elsewhere from which there would be no return, serve as a bridge to the contemporary diaspora. In literary terms, Arenas, with his Cuban beginnings and later off-island production, spans the distance from the canon to the diaspora, from Carpentier, to Obejas, to young writers whose work was never nourished by a Cuban landscape yet seeks to reconnect, free of the constraints of nostalgia and false memory, with the social, human, cultural, and historical experience of the island.

Chapter Two

Building the Cuban Canon: "Memories of the Future"

We have to name everything—everything that defines, envelops and surrounds us: everything that operates with the energy of *context*—in order to situate it within the universal.

—Alejo Carpentier, *Tientos y diferencias* (1967)

Los Recuerdos del Porvenir, (Memories of the Future), is the name of a tavern along the Orinoco River that appears, significantly, midway through Carpentier's novel *The Lost Steps* (*Los pasos perdidos,* 1953). In this book, Carpentier elaborates a theory of Latin American culture, subtly weaving it into the fabric of the novel without distracting from, or competing with, the narrative itself. Structured as an odyssey of return, the search for origins, for historical memory and the possibility of its reclaiming, is—as the name of the tavern suggests—intimately connected to a vision of the future and its realization.

Carpentier began writing in the 1930s. By the late 1940s and early 1950s, he was producing mature works to great international acclaim. It was in that decade or so, Raymond Souza argues, that Carpentier engaged in the process of "moving the Cuban novel from regionalistic to universal concerns."[1] In that study, Souza offers a comprehensive overview of twentieth-century Cuban literature as a framework for the study of three of its major figures. Souza cites 1959 to 1971 as one of the most prolific periods for novelistic production. Carpentier's mature novels, those that projected contemporary Cuban literature into the international arena, ushered in Cuba's twentieth-century golden age and were constructed with an invigorating will to liberation.

Carpentier often repeated the notion of the writer as namer of the world, comparing the enormous responsibility of the writer in Latin America with that of Adam. It was not so much a question of *naming* things as it was of *renaming* them in the process of revisiting history, which in turn was part of the larger project shared, to one degree or another, by all the "boom" writers. Freed from the restrictions imposed on the imagination by an ensemble of traditions inherited from Europe and assimilated without a critical and discriminating eye or intellect, Latin American literature could proceed to reclaim its place in the world. Nowhere is Carpentier's intent, as both novelist and theorist, clearer than in *The Lost Steps*. Unable to get out from under the weight of a poorly digested tradition, the narrator and would-be creator is defeated by it: "Every time I saw the members of a symphony orchestra seated behind their music racks, I waited impatiently for the moment when time should cease to pile up incoherent sounds and fall into an organized framework in response to a prior human will. . . . Inside the covers of the score were set down in signs the orders of men who, though dead in ornate mausoleums—or their bones lost in the dreary disorder of some potter's field—still held author's rights on time, imposing the measure of motion and emotion on future men."[2]

As alienated in Latin America as he is in his adopted New York landscape, the composer turned adman fails as an artist and as a human being. His is an odyssey that ultimately leads nowhere. In his quest for authenticity, he comes up empty-handed because he has been searching in all the wrong places, both outside and within himself. Yet the novel, in its detailed depiction of the myopia, alienation, and withdrawal of a transplanted Latin American artist, yields a powerful literary catharsis, a liberating force for the novel. To abandon all schema, to free oneself from the artist's subjugation or obeisance to the traditions that have gone before, from the potentially asphyxiating legacy of Western civilization: that is the dilemma that drives the narrator-protagonist of *The Lost Steps*. Through his successive displacements, from his Caribbean homeland to New York and back to Latin America—with the paradigm of Europe a constant framework for comparison—in search of "primitive" musical instruments to take back, as well as his own origins, Carpentier develops the problematic of the Latin American artist into the work's central theme. What stays with the reader of Carpentier's ambitious novel (ambitious in its theoretical reach and sheer ground covered) is not the abject failure of the protagonist in his quest for *lo auténtico latinoamericano* but rather the pathos and detailed rendering of the vicious circle in which he is caught. The battle between here and there, Europe and America, city and country, "civilization" and "chaos," in the mind of the narrator, a man who feels himself a prisoner of Western civilization (a concept of civilization he has a poor grasp of and is thus ill-prepared to define), bears down on him with the weight of a legion of dead men and paralyzes him. The dichotomy that structures his quest is a cul-de-sac. It reduces his constant movement across space and time to the eternal return of a pendulum that swings, inevitably, back in on itself.

The desire for escape, for a way out, does not necessarily signal decadence or defeatism; it may hold within itself the will, conscious or not, toward liberation. It all depends on the route taken, and the point of departure. For the Latin American romantic spirit, freedom was too often measured by the degree of success achieved in transposing to America the ideals and traditions of the "Western" world. For Carpentier's alienated antihero, the West rises up as a set of traditions that oblige the creator to heed them, to submerge himself in them, like a Hamlet who, in spite of himself, turns his back on the world around him and obeys only the will of his dead father. The European tradition that fed the romantics' longing for freedom constitutes, for Carpentier's protagonist, at mid–twentieth century, a kind of straitjacket. For him, the quest for "freedom" means going to Latin America, but his is an ahistorical, formless Latin America, more dream than reality. He inverts the equation that subordinates Latin America to the dream of Europe, but the relation remains a fixed equation simply turned on its head, incapable of perceiving and reflecting change, of confronting and incorporating dialectically a fluid present undergoing constant transformation.

In a 1967 essay titled *Tientos y diferencias: Problemática actual de la novela latinoamericana,* Carpentier articulated his novelistic theory. He challenged those who decried the imminent demise of the novel. His refutation took the form of enumerating and defining all the possibilities still to be explored in the contemporary Latin American novel, alluding to future directions. As a corrective to the dead end of the psychological novel with its small characters, he proposed the richness and validity of the novel of great historical movements, whose characters transcend the limitations of the form by inserting themselves within what he termed "contexts." These contexts—cultural, culinary, historical, architectural—are the multiple facets of ambient reality within which the men and women who populate the novel move, and in relation to which they define themselves. The compendium of contexts makes up the culture of every nation, and for Carpentier, the history of a nation's cultural development *is* that nation's history.

Grounding in concrete history is another fundamental aspect of Carpentier's novelistic theory. He sticks close to historical document, branching out from it in all directions in the elaboration of the novel to achieve an expansive synthesis. In his oeuvre, we encounter a realist content expressed in baroque style, the only style adequate, he argued, to recreate and make intelligible a Latin American reality that had not been exploited in literature. The baroque, in style and form, corresponded essentially to the Latin American, Caribbean, content of his work. Only through the baroque was it possible to describe a *ceiba,* as opposed to a pine tree. The need to name, to define, and create a universe palpable to the reader was a requisite for all works whose sources and frame of reference originated outside of Europe, beyond the metropolis.

The related concepts of the marvelous-real and "New World" syncretism originated in two of Carpentier's own journeys: one to Haiti, and the other to the Amazon, along the Orinoco. The course of the Orinoco, into the jungle, corresponds to the flow of historical time. Traveling the river, the novelist encountered cities that seemed frozen in the Middle Ages alongside "modern" European-style cities, until he reached the heart of the Amazon, a symbolic return to the matrix. This, then, served as the basis for *The Lost Steps.* Haiti, with its marked historical cycles, revolutionary tradition, and mythology, is identified with Carpentier's concept of history as spiral, a concept that directly informs *The Kingdom of This World* and *Explosion in a Cathedral,* as well as the rest of his novels, to one degree or another. The epigraph that opens *Explosion in a Cathedral* is the key to understanding the spiral of history, the revolutionary impulse across generations and continents, and the importance of faith implicit in his vision: "Las palabras no caen al vacío." The phrase presupposes an unbreakable faith in humanity's struggle to transform reality, to achieve justice, if not in one lifetime, for the generations to come. Carpentier believes that to understand the present, our present, and insert ourselves fully within it, we must all become students of history. Only then can we understand the ways in which the French Revolution is related to Caribbean history, extending to contemporary initiatives and concerns, or see the connections that stretch from the October revolution to the Spanish civil war and the Cuban revolution of 1959. The sudden illumination of such historical connections within Latin American reality is the marvelous-real as it functions in Carpentier's *Kingdom of This World, Explosion in a Cathedral,* and *Consagración de la primavera.*

Carpentier constructs his novels on a double axis—the spatial, here/there, and the temporal, now/then—to achieve a synthesis capable of revealing the contrast between values imposed from the outside, from the textual space of Europe, and autochthonous American values. *The*

Harp and the Shadow (*El arpa y la sombra,* 1979), Carpentier's counter-biography of Columbus, is extremely important for elucidating the basis for his theory because it forces the reader to revisit the first collision of European values and indigenous American values in the "discovery" of America.

The Lost Steps puts the marvelous-real to work on the spatial axis through the displacements of an urban musicologist who travels the Amazon in search of his own Latin American roots under the pretext of bringing back the "primitive" instruments he is being funded to collect. The alienated narrator-protagonist is the connective thread of the novel, like Victor Hughes in *Explosion in a Cathedral,* and his geographical movements serve to juxtapose and contrast here and there, there and here, creating a syncretic canvas composed of the multiple layers of American reality. *The Lost Steps* is the final version of the problem of return, telluric and intellectual, posited earlier in "Journey Back to the Source." The musicologist attempts an escape from his New York world, one he now finds both alienated and alienating, by heading for Latin America in search of authentic values. The cosmopolitan women in his life—Ruth, his wife, and Mouche, his mistress—embody the false values he hopes to cast off, just as Rosario, the *mestiza* lover he takes on the journey, sums up for him the authenticity to which he aspires. All three female characters are necessarily stereotypical, functioning as symbols that chart the musicologist's quest rather than three-dimensional characters in their own right. The narrator also experiences a mythological trajectory during the course of which he sheds the role of Sisyphus, assumes the identity of Prometheus, and later Ulysses, only to resume his lot as Sisyphus at the novel's conclusion. He is a failed man on all accounts, condemned to eternal isolation, to individual labor that goes nowhere and results in nothing.

El acoso (1963), a tale of Havana, set in the period of student-led revolutionary uprisings in the city, also takes failure, one young man's aborted attempt at liberation, as its theme. His growing isolation from the larger collective movement around him is the cause of his undoing. Every event within the narrative takes place in Havana, yet there is a subtle contrast between city and countryside, since the protagonist is a scholarship student from a small town. Although once again based on historical document, on real events in the city's history, the narrative structure is not chronological, following instead the back-and-forth swings of the protagonist's consciousness, the confused chain of associations in the mind of a student turned informer. After entering the university, the protagonist joins the Communist Party and begins a theoretical apprenticeship that should have guided him toward praxis. Unlike *The Lost Steps,* in *El acoso* the protagonist's failure is due not to escapism but to impatience. After ripping up his party card, he abandons the university as well to join a group of impatient young men who have formed a splinter group. They carry out a series of violent, ill-fated missions designed to precipitate the government's collapse rather than work within an organized movement and let history take its course. The impatient young man's tragic failure and ultimate death bring us back to the epigraph from Zohar in *Explosion in a Cathedral,* a novel of the grand collective movements of history favored by Carpentier.

Explosion in a Cathedral also takes Havana as its point of departure, specifically, the home of three well-off young siblings who have shut themselves up in it following the death of their father. Events of the French Revolution and its repercussions in the Caribbean are narrated through the adventures and misadventures of the novel's four characters. In studying the Age of Enlightenment, Carpentier came upon a potentially significant figure, one whose life and role in the Revolution were only scantly documented. Victor Hughes's life serves as the novel's framework. In the process of putting all the pieces together and recreating that life, across space and time, from France to the Caribbean, the raw material for the novel emerged. Hughes appears one day in the Havana home of the young trio, with their grand, humanitarian ideals of Revolution, and propels them into action. At the novel's center lies the image of the *caracol,* the snail, with its spiral-like form. The symbol of the spiral is the philosophical core from which all of Carpentier's novels emanate. It suggests, here, the ultimate meaning of the contradictory and ironic Age of Enlightenment. In the novel's second half, the siblings leave Havana for Europe in order to gain an understanding of the origins of a movement that is resonating throughout the Caribbean. Although the characters distance themselves from their Cuban homeland, the novel itself never loses sight of the Caribbean. Behind every pulse, twist, and turn the novel takes lies the idea that the Caribbean will be the site from which the next revolutionary movement will emerge. That it has stagnated in France, once institutionalized, does not mean that all is lost. The possibility of a renewed and more rigorous campaign for change lies just around the next curve in Carpentier's historical spiral.

The young characters, who appeared infinitely malleable at the outset, acquire identity as the text's full range unfolds: Esteban, as the theoretician of the revolution; Victor Hughes, as the "man of action," blunted by constant activity untempered by reflection, and blinded by his own recourse to brute force; Sofía, as praxis, the ideal balance of theory and a practice, acquired over time, and molded by accumulated experience. At the novel's end, her brother Carlos will clearly return to the Caribbean to pick up where Sofía left off.

Explosion in a Cathedral narrates the French Revolution from a Caribbean perspective, in the same way that *The Harp and the Shadow* narrates the "discovery" of America from the inside outward, from an American perspective. In Carpentier's oeuvre, as in his biography, the European experience is ever present yet tempered by Latin American reality, examined through a Latin American prism.

In Carpentier's mature novelistic production, we find twentieth-century Cuban literature's full thematic range: chronicles of alienation as well as chronicles of liberation, all centered on what it means to be Cuban in the world, in dialectical relation to Europe, Latin America, and the rest of the Caribbean. His characters travel the globe, journey within themselves, into the past and toward the future, engaged in the project of fully understanding the present they inhabit. Carpentier's themes, with their constant motion and dialectical approach to culture, stand out as the strongest and most immediate link to contemporary Cuban-American voices engaged in an inquiry into their surroundings, their own off-island reality and the task of separating out the received ideas and mythology that may have contaminated historical interpretation.

My discussion of the Cuban canon in these pages is necessarily partial. I have selected major works whose themes are being elaborated in a different context, that of current Cuban-American narrative, forming a bridge. Many masters have obviously been omitted, not for lack of merit but out of consideration for the structuring motifs of this study, highlighting thematic commonality in Cuban writing on and off the island.

José Lezama Lima, one of twentieth-century Cuban narrative's most original and challenging figures, however, cannot be left out. His impact on contemporary letters and international literary studies has not abated. In fact, following his rehabilitation on the island, Lezama Lima is presently enjoying a renaissance, and the Casa José Lezama Lima, an institute dedicated to his life and work, was established in 1994.[3] Known to scholars of Cuban literature in the 1940s and 1950s for his editorship of the journal *Orígenes* (1944–1956), the poet Lezama Lima received international attention for his novel *Paradiso* in 1966. His dense, rich, baroque novel continues to generate dissertations and make work for scholars. This chapter will not attempt yet another interrogation of *Paradiso;* to place it in context, acknowledging the major space it has carved out for itself within the canon as well as its influence on the trajectory of Cuban narrative of the last three decades will suffice. I am admittedly dancing around the edges of one of Cuban literature's most difficult and rewarding masterworks. In handwritten notes found among his papers, Lezama Lima himself stated that *"Paradiso* will be understood in a realm beyond reason."[4] Cuban novelist Reynaldo González views the challenges the text poses more as invitation to playful collaboration than intimidation: "I know readers of Lezama who don't understand him—really, all of his readers doubt if we have understood him—but enjoy the playful flexibility of language that can take them on an unlimited poetic adventure."[5]

Lezama Lima began the nearly 500-page novel of the Cemí family, a parody of origins, in the mid–nineteen fifties and published the work in its entirety in 1966. In an interview conducted in 1970, Lezama Lima commented on what the novel represented in terms of his entire oeuvre: "After the Revolution, its general conception and cosmic meaning were completed. That is to say, the conception encompasses the pre-revolutionary periods; and the completion, its emergence, occurred at the same time that the Revolution was taking shape, acquiring form" (quoted in Simón, 19–20; translation mine).

Centered on the figure of the adolescent José Cemí, *Paradiso* is a novel of the destiny of one Cuban family with many branches, and of the protagonist's movement from multiplicity to unity. Chronologically, the story moves from the closing years of the nineteenth century to the 1930s in "a continual process of expansion" (Souza 1976, 55).

Raymond Souza compares Lezama Lima to James Joyce for the degree of his complexity but reminds us of a significant difference in the origins and contours of that textual complexity: "Lezama Lima's work is as much an affirmation of one cultural context as Joyce's is a denial of another" (Souza 1976, 53).

An exploration of origins within one family, an inquiry into their ultimate significance and of meaning in the past, *Paradiso* is also a construction of history through image and symbol. The baroque density of the work arises from an elemental recognition of Cuban culture from the very beginning, and a desire to fill the voids. José Rodríguez Feo, one of the founding members of the Orígenes group, attributes to the novel's baroque density a compensatory function: "In *Paradiso* you could say that the imagination has avenged itself on a reality impoverished by

underdevelopment, by constructing a world in which Lezama participates in and enjoys all the cultural wealth that has up until now been
reserved for the people of more civilized societies. . . . There is no doubt
that if Lezama had written within the framework of a society that was
not underdeveloped, his work would not present that obsession with
things cultural, and he would approach reality from a completely different point of reference" (quoted in Simón, 328; translation mine).

The masterful use of baroque style to express a profoundly Cuban
content is one of the many parallels that may be drawn between Carpentier and Lezama Lima, yet there are overwhelming differences at the
level of text and context between these two seminal figures. Both have a
philosophical and writerly concern with *process,* with the influence the
past exerts on the present and the shaping of the future. Souza, who
devotes a chapter to each of them in *Major Cuban Novelists,* identifies a
fundamental difference in the two novelists' approach to the same set of
philosophical, cultural, and social problems: "Carpentier finds solace in
man's collective unconscious and Lezama Lima in the hermetic image"
(Souza 1976, 78).

Yet both are concerned more with the philosophical process of
becoming than with outcome, interested more in change, creation, and
transformation in human existence and destiny than in preserving what
came before. Hence the spiral in the configuration of Carpentier's novels, and the spiraling movement of historical becoming in *Paradiso,* as
well. For Souza, "Reading the novel is like tracing the course of several
spirals as they move through time and space and slowly come together"
(Souza 1976, 58).

Carpentier escaped the suffocating atmosphere of the 1950s, inhos-
pitable to historical fiction, to the attempt to create anything other than
an "asocial, evasive, ultrarefined literature,"[6] and Lezama Lima stayed
and faced it down. Together they extended the limits of the fictional
universe. Lezama Lima's novel ends with the phrase "now we can
begin," suggesting the complicity of an engaged reader, the dialectic of
history, the need to go back to the beginning for a closer second reading,
or perhaps all three imperatives. *Paradiso* is immense. One submits to its
power as if to the flow of history, of the life force itself, or as Souza affec-
tionately and succinctly puts it: "The world is not quite so terrifying
after having read *Paradiso,* for the novel encourages its readers to see life
in its totality" (Souza 1976, 76).

Historical inquiry and displacement have been vehicles for the literary journey of self-discovery in our century, which received a strong ini-

tial impetus from 1920 to 1930, when the republic took a long, hard look at itself. "Cuba was discovered by Columbus in the fifteenth century; by the Cuban intelligentsia in the nineteenth century, what was left was for Cuba to discover itself and that was what happened in this period."[7]

The structure and aesthetics of *la novela-testimonio,* or testimonial novel, furthered the goal of self-discovery as an expression of cultural autonomy. The testimonial novel arose in the 1960s from the ashes of the chronicles of the conquerors. This time around, the texts constitute a chronicle of the vanquished of Latin America. In the climate of the 1960s, in which everything was being revisited, reappraised, and in which thought and action were once again wedded on campus and off, throughout Europe and the Americas, testimonial narratives brought readers and writers closer together. The form itself presupposed active readership; *testimonio* required readers to insert themselves within the historical epoch being revisited. It made of the reader one more of the book's characters. Miguel Barnet, one of the pioneers of the genre in the 1960s, posited a reader who would be "moving, gesticulating, judging. . . . with a margin of freedom to contradict or affirm."[8]

Many of the testimonial novels of the 1960s were Cuban: Barnet's *Biografía de un cimarrón* (1966), which has just been reissued on its 30th anniversary in a facsimile edition, and his *Canción de Rachel* (1969), Renée Méndez Capote's *Memorias de una cubanita que nació con el siglo* (1964), and Reinaldo Arenas's *El mundo alucinante* (1969). Edmundo Desnoes's *Memorias del subdesarrollo* (1965) and Pablo Armando Fernández's *Los niños se despiden* (1968), though not strictly *novelas testimonio,* have much in common with the genre.

Either exalted or suppressed, the *yo* (the *I*) of these narratives is moving from *estar,* the sense of being in context, historical and geographical, to *ser,* being in an ontological sense. Rootedness, the roots that ground us, and the search for the root causes of a given set of problems, make up the dominant thematic in this grouping of novels, if not in the contemporary Cuban novel in general. Testimonial novels lend additional force to the quest by casting off the official framework of history, blurring the boundaries of fiction and history, fiction and reality, to uncover new sources of meaning.

Pablo Armando Fernández's novel *Los niños se despiden* (1968) is structured as a series of poetic familial tales, a collage of narrative voices. Fernández was a disciple of Lezama Lima, and the novel is a baroque torrent of words in which individual streams of consciousness alternate, mingle, and merge into collective history. Images of *el jardín* (the garden) alternate with others throughout the text, recasting it as seed, tree, *ceiba*. The family saga begins at the end, with the gate that opens onto the gardens, the street, the passersby, all the elements that configure a new destiny. In this individual and collective coming-of-age tale, the children of the title must open the gate and say good-bye to sterile innocence, to the confinement of their class. A preoccupation with history and language informs the novel. In its unfolding, history will become dynamic, ceasing to be the monotonous recitation of geography and predetermination, the static contemplation of the father: "What had to be loved and respected, to say it in family terms, was geography. We had a very poor concept of history; we were ahistorical. The important thing was being Cuban, feeling Cuban, and that could only be determined by our geography, its climate and nature. We were Cuban because we had been born here and not somewhere else, in the same way that the Galicians were Galician, the Moors, Moors, and the Polish, Polish."[9]

The language of the novel, in the development and trajectory of each of the characters, reflects their attitude toward change, either fluid, dynamic, and open, or a stagnant accumulation of the preconceived and predetermined. Revolution, the possibility and project of societal change, requires a new language, and acquisition of that new language within the novel is a form of reappropriating and reinterpreting history.

> There is nothing as enjoyable as hearing all the people speaking that strange, new language, full of abbreviations and words that have lost their true image and which, by repeating them and using them up the way they do, will leave them without a single syllable in one piece. But people are also learning much wiser things. I can't get bogged down in this business of the new words, as seductive as they are. There is nothing superior to words, or more beautiful, or stronger, or more vital, or eternal. In the Beginning was the spoken word, and at the End, the written word, and everyone has learned to write and read. So we will spend our lives in Sabanas writing and reading, reading and writing books that tell our own history and our own life from Beginning to End, full of words. (*Los niños,* 269; translation mine)

The novels of the realist strain of the 1960s, though distinct in style, register the same urgency of odyssey and movement as the dense, baroque narratives of Lezama Lima, Carpentier, and Pablo Armando Fernández.

Two significant works of that decade, Renée Méndez Capote's *Memorias de una cubanita que nació con el siglo* (1964) and Edmundo Desnoes's *Memorias del subdesarrollo* (1965), explore the interior and exterior worlds of the Cuban bourgeoisie, the latter in the development of the republic at the turn of the century and the former in the early years of the revolution. Although both cast their glance back at what was, neither of these texts constitutes a narrative of nostalgia. Méndez Capote's text is a *despedida,* a farewell. It opens with a rebel's cry and closes with the bitter aftertaste of disillusionment, as the reality of the republic, by then in its adolescence, sinks in.

> I was born immediately before the Republic. I in November of 1901, and she in May of 1902; but from birth we were different: she was born amended and I was born determined never to allow myself to be amended.[10]

In an interview I conducted with Renée Méndez Capote in the mid-1980s, she described the process of writing *Memorias* as that of a long, sustained cry of liberation. After the fall of Batista, Méndez Capote, from an illustrious, progressive Cuban family, threw herself into the social programs of the revolution, primarily the literacy and adult-education campaigns. Her husband grew jealous, she explained, but it was not a lover distancing her from him but her social activism. *Memorias* was her first new work since 1927. It is a rich, contradictory catharsis, both of gender and class restrictions; in it she evokes and recreates the world in which she was formed, in meticulous, clear-eyed detail and with particular emphasis on consumption. All that was worn, eaten, drunk, listened to, and read by her class, the bourgeoisie, is inventoried, providing the contours of an epoch, its history. For Christmas Eve of 1912, for example, there were "black beans. And *turrones,* and raisins in big boxes with cheerful girls on the lids, and dates that really came all the way from Smirna, . . . And ham from Galicia, several kinds of French and Dutch cheeses and tins of butter from the Trappist fathers, and quince and marzipan from Toledo, *sobreasada* from the Sierra and sausages from Vich. Sparkling wine, and white wine, and red wine, Italian, German and French. Asturian cider and Moet and Chandon champagne" (*Memorias de una cubanita,* 184; translation mine). Alternating with the dizzying imported abundance of bourgeois consumption are the descriptions of *la política,* the unresolved conflicts constantly erupting within the republic, from the perspective of an observant child, one who is gaining the use of reason and determined to stand on her own.

In 1907, now six years old, the narrator discovers the social world beyond the home. "Around that time, people began to exist. The world began to populate itself" (*Memorias de una cubanita,* 27; translation mine). And soon after that, she confronts injustice, in the form of "those Spanish wet nurses who left their own children behind in Spain and came to Cuba to bring up, for money, little Cuban children without mothers" (189; translation mine).

Occasional historical flashbacks to the period of the independence wars offer a glimpse into the origins of the bourgeoisie of the republic: "It is Havana, 1869. War has just broken out and the rich, aristocratic and pro-slavery, who have amassed their wealth and purchased their titles with the suffering of Blacks, don't give a damn whether Cuba ever becomes free" (*Memorias de una cubanita,* 95; translation mine).

The Méndez Capote family is as bourgeois as the next but stands on the opposing side of the political divide. Nationalist and staunchly separatist, friend to the Puerto Rican poet and *independentista,* Lola Rodríguez de Tío, they are nonetheless steeped in European culture and contemptuous of the United States: "The Cuban society of my childhood was formed in Europe. Anything North American was looked down upon as barbaric and of inferior quality" (*Memorias de una cubanita,* 151; translation mine).

The narrator's passage from infancy to puberty in this climate parallels the development of the truncated republic, from expectation to disillusionment in one decade. No amount of French wines and imported European delicacies suffices to fill the void. Thus the novel ends on a bitter note of frustration. Renecita's emotional awakening, the first stirrings of love, or rather infatuation, is a thinly veiled reference to the republican experience, the Cuban nationalists' brief love affair with the idea and symbol of the republic, one that ended in frustration and stasis: "It was a love affair very much of its time; made up of vague glances and smiles, of him passing back and forth on horseback in front the house while I remained seated without daring to move so much as a finger" (*Memorias de una cubanita,* 191; translation mine).

Like Lezama Lima's *Paradiso,* Edmundo Desnoes's *Memorias del subdesarrollo* (published in English as *Inconsolable Memories*) is a novel that does not cross borders. It is a Cuban narrative of *staying,* in this case of one man's decision to stay behind and confront his own underdevelopment and that of his class while those that had formed the very texture of his life depart for Miami, New York, and Paris to continue the dream of "otherness," of foreign schooling and foreign wines, that they grew up on. The narrator-protagonist of the novel believes, like Fuentes's Artemio Cruz, that his birth in Cuba was the result of an existential-geographical error, that he was destined to be a European. Having inherited numerous apartment buildings, now nationalized, he is rescued from his fate as a furniture salesman by the checks that arrive monthly as compensation. Fortuitously freed from the burdens of petit bourgeois family and business life, his decision to remain behind in a revolution he did nothing to bring about is impulsive, an existential lark. The revolution, with the monthly stipends it bestows, grants him a second chance at life, an entrée to the bohemian existence he is anxious to experience. Hard cynicism, rather than nostalgia, characterizes his attitude toward the past, the life he led up until days or moments ago. His monologue begins by tearing apart wife, family, and colleagues, pulling off the facade, layer by layer, of the artificially constructed Cuban bourgeoisie: "I'm glad, because it was all a big farce: I wasn't interested in my wife's taste in clothes, and I don't love my parents very much, and being the Simmons representative here in Cuba (I wasn't born to make or sell furniture) left me cold, and all my friends managed to do was bore me stiff."[11]

So he stays, not to take any part in the transformation of society but to remain detached from it in the top-floor apartment from which he gazes down on society's movement through binoculars set up on the balcony. His purpose is to write, from the position of his new "freedom-solitude." The self-involved diary-chronicle that the narrator pecks away at on a manual typewriter, between naps and halfhearted seductions, *is* the novel. He fails, finding that not only does he have nothing to do to fill his days, but he has nothing to say. Yet along the way, Desnoes exposes, like an X-ray diagram, the heart of the disaffected bourgeoisie, its insularity, the trappings of the colonized mind à la Havana in the 1960s, while the protagonist appropriates the surface, the catchphrases, of European existentialism as justification for his own inertia.

The text is peppered with references to fashionable readings of the day—Hemingway, Lao-tzu, and Neruda, and Stendhal and Montaigne from the French literary canon. But what obsesses the narrator is a line from the film *Hiroshima, mon amour,* a line that represents for him the sum total of all the civilization lacking in Cuba, positing a romantic sensibility bordering on nihilism. This, then, is his simple answer to what he believes to be the inherent underdevelopment of the tropics: " *J'ai désiré avoir une inconsolable mémoire.'* I suspect civilization is just that: knowing how to relate things, not forgetting anything. That's why civilization is impossible here: Cubans easily forget the past: they live too much in the present" (*Inconsolable,* 37). Through his interior monologues, the reader sees *what* the narrator sees and *how* he sees it, journeying with him into growing isolation and alienation from both past and present: "Thirty-nine years and I'm already old. I don't feel any wiser, as an Oriental philosopher would expect, not even riper. A dried-up mango, bagasse. . . . Maybe it has something to do with the tropics. Everything ripens and rots easily here. Nothing endures like the taste of cod liver oil. A regular habitué of the Havana brothels when I was thirteen. At fifteen I thought I was a genius. At twenty-two, the owner of a sophisticated furniture store. My life is like a monstrous, spongy, tropical vegetable. Enormous leaves and no fruit" (103).

He daydreams of atomic obliteration, of the fragility of life and the immortality conferred by an inconsolable memory, until a real crisis, the Missile Crisis of 1962, emerges with its potential for real and imminent destruction: "You can imagine a shot, being stabbed by a knife, the explosion of a grenade. I can't visualize the city of Havana destroyed, evaporated by a hydrogen bomb. . . . What I feel, what I'm going through is meaningless when confronted by the facts. *Nada.* Everything seems out of proportion. We here, and the rest of the world. Nuclear energy and my small apartment. Everything is out of proportion" (*Inconsolable,* 142–43). The shock of recognition that he is part of that *we* that would be destroyed jolts the protagonist into letting go of idées fixes, old patterns, even the ideal of an inconsolable memory that he no longer desires: "This diary is useless. Underdevelopment and civilization. Never learn. I take myself too seriously. . . . If they drop the bomb, if we survive. My head. No, I don't want it. Makes no difference. It's a lie, it does make a difference. I do care" (152–53).

Having learned to view his own world, and to reduce it, the way an outsider would, he is suddenly struck by its awesome complexity, at the very center of global conflict. His early playing at existential crisis, the petit bourgeois's answer to ennui in the form of a diary, evolves into a profound, transformative existential crisis, triggered within the protagonist by the Missile Crisis, which connects him inescapably, because of his decision to stay on the island, to history and collective destiny. The resolution of his personal existential crisis lies beyond the closing phrase of the text, "Man (I) is sad, but wants to live. . . . Go beyond words" (*Inconsolable,* 154).

Can the protagonist face the convulsive society around him, which he finally begins to understand, in ways that will not render meaningless his impulsive decision not to leave? Can he find new definitions for the concepts of freedom and dignity, or at least learn to formulate the questions differently?

Reinaldo Arenas's *El mundo alucinante* (1969), the last work to be examined in this chapter, is yet another set of "memories of the future," a quest for identity in the present through the telescoping of time into America's past. The novel is based on the life, times, and published memoirs of Fray Servando Teresa de Mier, a historical figure who would have celebrated his 200th birthday at the time of the book's publication. Servando embodies the ongoing quest for liberation and the right to self-representation around the time of Latin America's independence movements. Fray Servando is thus a product of the Age of Enlightenment, a late-eighteenth-century *criollo.* Through him, we are exposed to all the forces of change in the air at the time, an apt venue for exploring the forces of change operating in the 1960s in Cuba, and throughout the continent. A highly contradictory figure—a nobleman who chooses to pursue one of the most contemptible occupations—Mier is at once victim and oppressor, provoking his own incarceration so that he can devise forms of liberation. Through his displacements, from America to Europe and back, like the protagonists in Carpentier's *Explosion in a Cathedral* and *Concierto barroco,* Arenas examines what it means to be American in a shifting world. Mier bumps into prominent cultural figures of the time, and his dialogues with Cuban romantic poet Heredia in *El mundo alucinante* explore the individuality and narrative voice of the writer. Their exchanges contemplate the Latin American *I,* searching for freedom through movement, journey, and literary expression. Arenas states expressly that his goal is to place Fray Servando in the text the *way* he is and as *what* he is: one of the most important and, sadly, one of the least-known figures of the literary and political history of America. The preface to the work, written as a letter from the author to Fray Servando, explains: "The most useful things, for getting to know you and love you, were not the overwhelming encyclopedias, always too exact, or the terrible books of essays, always too inexact. The most valuable thing was discovering that you and I are the same person."[12]

Arenas rejected all historical documentation, relying only on Servando Teresa de Mier's own two-volume *Memorias* as guide, citing them often, "not as quotes from a foreign text, but as a fundamental part" of his own (re)creation (*El mundo,* 9; translation mine).

Servando's travel commentaries, moving from Mexico to Europe, across Spain, France, Italy, Portugal, and England, then back to America via the United States, Mexico, and Cuba, before returning, ultimately, to his point of origin in Mexico, allow for the juxtaposition of "old" and "new" worlds in the shaping of an American identity. Servando's adventures are episodes in a historical campaign to make American reality known, breaking out of the Old World–New World equation of civilization versus barbarism, as the friar's eloquent lament at the center of the text makes clear: "For how long will the fact of being American constitute a condemnation, a sentence that can only be lifted by years of exile and the polishing action of foreign and often useless cultures? For how long will we be considered paradisiacal and lascivious, creatures of sun and water?" (*El mundo,* 105; translation mine).

A cultural and political activist, Servando rejected the contemplative life on principle. For him, thought and meditation divorced from action are ineffective. Toward the end of his days, as he is about to sit down to write, he is interrupted by visitors seeking guidance. He advises that "the best way to knowledge is through living" (*El mundo,* 219; translation mine).

Later, as he is about to read, he stops to contemplate his hands, symbol of action throughout the text. There follows a lengthy poetic soliloquy on *estas manos* (these hands). In it, he looks back over a lifetime of action, guided by thought, traveling back over the course of his life in the moments before it is to end. The narrative's affirmation of New World values is arrived at and reinforced through Servando's travels, his repeated contact with, and deepening knowledge of, the Old World.

Servando's adventures, his constant displacements through exile and self-exile, do not cease even with death. When the liberal party triumphs, taking possession of churches and convents, the cadavers of 13 friars are removed from their sepulchres and left exposed to the elements; among them is Fray Servando's. Purchased by an Italian, his remains travel to Buenos Aires, where the director of a circus exhibits them as those of a victim of the Inquisition. The narrative closes with a report of the cadaver having last been spotted in Belgium.

Arenas's recreation of the life of a globe-trotting Mexican friar raises important questions of historical interpretation and cultural practice in the making of Latin America at a time when Cuban society was in the process of remaking itself. Miguel Barnet's series of *novelas-testimonio,* begun in the 1960s as well, redress a skewed interpretation of the nation's history and serve as compass points in the reorienting of Cuban narrative.

Chapter Three
Canon and Diaspora:
A Literary Dialogue

Sameness is sublimated difference;
Diversity is accepted difference.

—Édouard Glissant, *Caribbean Discourse* (1989)

Rapprochement

The testimonial novel in Latin America has had an impact on historiography and fictional narrative. One of the important shifts it contributed to was that of exploding the false unity imposed from above by the Creole elite, exposing the diverse visions and versions of history as it was experienced by indigenous Afro-Latin Americans and women, all the groups who fought and built the nation-state only to be denied full citizenship within its development. One may read in *testimonios* such as *Autobiography of a Runaway Slave* a direction that, according to Neil Larsen, "points to the development of a new social and epic realism, cleared of the bourgeois master narratives of nationalism, populism, masculinism."[1]

This chapter will look at contemporary Cuban and Cuban-American narratives as they intertwine, signaling the potential for even greater rapprochement in the twenty-first century. In the 1990s, Cuban-American writing increasingly seeks to explore issues of false memory in the construction of identity off the island in much the same ways that Cuban *testimonios* of the 1960s did from within.

Memory, history, and historiography are all intimately connected in testimonial literature. History, as it is remembered by the individuals and communities who lived it, and historiography—the skeleton, the structure, to be fleshed out—raise the question, *for* and *by whom?* Tensions and distortions are revealed in *testimonio* when individual and collective memories are put together, confronting one another; a multitude of voices is needed to sort out events. This holds as true for the social construction of Cuban identity in Miami, Chicago, or New York, now into its second and third generations, as it does for the discourse of the Cuban nation. For that reason, although each work stands complete, with its own structural coherence, Angel Fernández Guerra argues that *Autobiography of a Runaway Slave* and *Rachel's Song* may be read as a continuum: "Esteban Montejo's narrative encompassed the last years of the colony; in the specific case of the informant, the passage includes, in order: slavery, maroonage, patronage and the Independence War. Rachel takes up where he leaves off, from the Republic up to the marasmus of the *machadato,* in which so many things caved in, including the Alhambra [theater]."[2]

With the directness and force of unadorned speech, Montejo's narrative fills in chapters of undocumented Cuban history, the pages written by Afro-Cubans that the Creole elite of the new republic would later deny. Rachel's testimony, that of a minor "artist" in a marginal theater, a cabaret, is contradictory, evasive, and fragmented. Montejo's narrative is expansive, broadening the parameters of Cuban history and its interpretive possibilities, whereas Rachel's is confining, reductionist, and alienated. To allow ourselves, as readers, to be carried through history on the flow of her words, as we did with Montejo, is, as Fernández Guerra comments in his study of both works, "to get lost" (535; translation mine). It is no wonder, then, that Barnet chose as the epigraph—and warning—for *Rachel's Song* the following phrase from Baudelaire: "How small is the world in the eyes of memory." We are not to trust her testimony.

Montejo, a reliable witness whose accounts are verified and, wherever possible, documented by anthropologist-compiler Barnet, pieces together the undocumented history of the social life of the slave barracks, and the life of the maroons, as well as that of the rural peasantry. Through his memories of more than a century of life, Montejo, in collaboration with Barnet, reconstructs the central role that Cubans of African ancestry played in the independence war, and another window opens onto the history of the nation. Montejo's memoir is a rich accumulation of data—traditions, customs, events previously unrecorded—which he states matter-of-factly, without interpretive slant, confident of the historical importance of what he is recounting. Rachel's memoir, in contrast, is *all* interpretive slant to camouflage the poverty of content, as well as her inability to place herself within historical context. She neither possesses nor desires a grasp of history: "This island is something special. The strangest, most tragic things have happened here. And it will always be that way. The earth, like human kind, has its destiny. And Cuba's destiny is mysterious."[3]

A discreet prostitute, surviving on society's fringes, she believes herself to be solidly middle-class and wraps herself in the flag of the Cuban nation, symbolically and literally, in her act with the circus troupe Las Maravillas de Austria. Rachel, however, becomes a reliable witness to the degree that her own internal contradictions mirror the lies the Cuban republic told itself. At a key point in the text, Rachel's version is corrected by that of Montejo. Both informants interpret the origins of the Little War of 1912. According to Rachel: "That was the Negroes' little war, the racist rumpus of 1912. Because of that I don't think the Negro can be given much more freedom. They were going to impose themselves here if it hadn't been for the government's good sense" (*Rachel's Song,* 53).

For Montejo, it was a struggle that went to the very core of the nation. The outcome of that war was to determine the trajectory of Cuba itself, either continuing the spirit of grassroots democracy that reigned briefly during a campaign that included Montejo, or squashing that spirit and excluding him from the nation-building project. Montejo's interpretation puts into question the very basis of the republic that Rachel has come to represent: "Since when in this country has a program more democratic than that of the Independents of Color been brought before the people than when we fought tooth and nail to gain benefits for us Negroes, who had come out of the war barefooted and in rags, hungry, just like Quintín Banderas, who was killed later while he was getting water from the well in his house? Let's not hear any more cheap talk" (*Rachel's Song,* 58). An anonymous opposing testimony follows, affirming Montejo's version and denouncing Rachel and the republic as one and the same: "Rachel is the best example of prostitution, the vice and the lie wrapped in a red ribbon that reigned in this country" (59).

Rachel's "song" is the mythmaking apparatus of the republic, internalized within her consciousness, that Montejo's narrative within the narrative dismantles. It was the same mythmaking apparatus, at its height under Machado, that Carpentier sought to escape in the process of writing his first novel, *Écue-Yamba-Ó.* At that time, Carpentier expressed his belief that Afro-Cuban mythology and ritual constituted the only stronghold capable of maintaining the integrity of a cultural identity under siege, since "The Holy Spirit, venerated by the Cué, didn't admit Yankee hotdogs between its votive breads," and the *bongó* was an "antidote to Wall Street."[4]

In the face of a nation that seemed to be crumbling, undergoing a process of denationalization, Carpentier brandished a seemingly impenetrable collective memory untouched by mass media or the U.S. influence. *Écue-Yamba-Ó* was written in a Havana jail in 1927, and published abroad, in Madrid, in 1933. Although he later acknowledged the work's defects, in spirit and letter, it no doubt led him to the discovery of the marvelous-real and an overarching concern with re-elaborating history from a Latin Americanist perspective to rid it of centuries of distortion inherited from the earliest Old World chroniclers.

Critic Irlemar Chiampi has observed that "the Caribbean of *El siglo de las luces* evokes, deliberately, Latin America's point of departure, the site of encounter between Columbus and the natives, the axis for the Spanish Conquest's expansion across the New World, the center from which the entire political, racial and anthropological problematic radiates, represented by the Conquest of America in the history of the West."[5]

Carpentier, in this sense, saw his successive novels as an ensemble, an integral unit, with one work building on the other in the framing of a new historical consciousness that would be the inseparable companion to a new Latin American aesthetic: "If I had to write *El reino de este mundo, Los pasos perdidos, El siglo de las luces,* that is, all of my oeuvre over again, from 'Viaje a la semilla' on, I would do it all the same way, without taking out or adding a single comma" ("Carpentier sobre *El siglo,*" 57; translation mine).

Miguel Barnet views all his testimonial works as forming a similarly cohesive ensemble. The key factor is memory, as he stated in the prologue to *La vida real:* "Memory, as part of the imagination, has been the touchstone of this book. If I have recreated dramatic situations and real characters, it has been in full concordance with the key to my testimonial oeuvre."[6]

Memory, and the uses of memory, in the construction and self-representation of individual, nation, or enclave within a nation, is the unifying element for all the works of contemporary Cuban and Cuban-American literature examined in this chapter. The tricks of memory, when distorted and manipulated, and the possibility of reclaiming its more solid, fundamental sources, are the grounds for a new literary dialogue between canon and diaspora. It is not accidental that *memory* appears in so many of the titles, from *Memorias de una cubanita que nació con el siglo* and *Memorias del subdesarrollo,* written in Cuba in the 1960s, to

Memory Mambo by Cuban-American Achy Obejas, written in the United States in the 1990s. In all these narratives, false memory is an obstacle to be cleared from consciousness in order to start afresh, and lucid, reclaimed memory constitutes the path from the past to an engagement with present reality, filling in the lacunae and blind spots that hindered full *concientización.*

Clearly, memory is also a political category across the spectrum of works examined here, from Carpentier, Barnet, and Méndez Capote to Achy Obejas and the new voices of an engagé Cuban-American literature. In a chapter of his study *Literary Bondage: Slavery in Cuban Narrative,* William Luis examines what he terms "the politics of memory" in Miguel Barnet's *Autobiography of a Runaway Slave.* According to Luis, Barnet was not only challenging earlier histories that omitted any account of the social life of slaves in the barracks and that of the maroons in Cuba but attempting to "rewrite literary history by introducing images present in Cuban history that had remained unexplored in the literature of the past century."[7] Years after the publication of *The Autobiography of a Runaway Slave,* Barnet articulated the twofold impetus of that project, stating "that his work with Montejo filled in gaps in historiography and the novel" (Barnet, quoted in Luis 1990, 208). Barnet discusses the shared revelation of collective memory, one that flows from the informant to the listener-transcriber, and ultimately to the readers. Such breakthroughs in consciousness constitute for Barnet a phenomenon common to historiography *and* the novel: "There is the poetry, the mystery of this kind of work. And, clearly, that wide open door that allows one to penetrate into the collective conscience, into the we. The dream of the *gestor* of the documentary novel, that thirst for expansion, for knowledge and identity, was also Malinowsky's, Ortiz', Nina Rodríguez', and that of the French novelists of the nineteenth century" (207).

Windows and doors onto history are opened within *testimonio* and certain novels, and as Luis observes, a work such as *"The Autobiography of a Runaway Slave* dialogues with other works and historical moments" (Luis 1990, 209), setting in motion a rich resonance across epochs and literary genres.

Achy Obejas, whose short story and novel will open my discussion of contemporary off-island writing, is clearly engaged in a dialogue with the Cuban canon. Her debut collection's title story, "We Came All the Way from Cuba So You Could Dress like This?" positions itself as a counterpoint to Cuban-American narratives of nostalgia by confronting head-on the selective, partial rewriting of history under the heading of "things that can't be told." After invoking the taboo, Obejas proceeds to blast it wide open, telling all, revealing what it is that can't be told and why, and in so doing begins a journey, in the spirit of Carpentier, back to the source. In *Memory Mambo,* a complex, nuanced, and masterfully crafted novel, Obejas continues the journey, exploding false memory, nostalgia, and the mythology of exile along the way. In its entirety, the work is an extended exploration of the meaning of memory within the context of what it means to be Cuban for the diaspora of the late twentieth century. The novel achieves a definitive break with narratives of nostalgia and evocation. Its fearless and unmitigated interrogation of surrounding reality, *her* reality, that of the displaced Cubans of Chicago who live side by side with Puerto Ricans and Chicanos who hold contrasting views on Cuba, the United States, and the wider world, brings Obejas in line with the marvelous-real. Obejas shares Carpentier's unwavering commitment to question surrounding reality down to the very bottom layer, and Lezama Lima's insistence on Cuban literature's intimate relationship with *la realidad circundante,* whether it is Havana, Santiago, or Chicago. Obejas's close, knowing scrutiny of the local in *Memory Mambo,* with its slow accumulation of revealing detail, is what renders the narrative universal, in the best of the novelistic tradition.

The novel opens with an exploration of memory, raising pointed questions regarding the uses, misuses, and meaning of memory. In fact, the entire first chapter is an extended meditation on memory, insisting on the insoluble connection between memory and historical consciousness. It is memory that will determine how the individual situates himself or herself within the flow of history. This link between individual memory and historicity is manifest in the opening paragraph: "I've always thought of memory as a distinct, individual thing. I've read with curiosity about the large parts of our brains where memory resides— how these areas remain vital, as animated at seventy-five as at twenty-five years old. Scientists say that when we think we're losing our memory what's actually happening is that we've blocked or severed connections."[8]

The narrator, Juani Casas, intimates from the very beginning that if the individual's connections to the flow of history are "blocked" or "severed," distortion will reign, as is increasingly the case of the Cuban-Americans around her, the family and neighbors that make up the social fabric of her life. Their contaminated memories can spread, contagiously, the way the plague of forgetting spreads to the entire community in García Márquez's *One Hundred Years of Solitude.*

> I often wonder just how distinct my memories are. Sometimes I'm convinced they're someone else's recollections I've absorbed. I'm not talking about hooking into past lives, or other links established spiritually or psychically to other times. I'm not talking at all about suppressed memories. It's just that sometimes other lives lived right alongside mine interrupt, barge in on my senses, and I no longer know if I really lived through an experience or just heard about it so many times, or so convincingly, that I believed it for myself—became the lens through which it was captured, retold and shaped. (*Memory Mambo,* 9)

There is much in Obejas's narrative, and the historical, ontological, existential questions raised by her narrator, Juani, that places the work squarely within the trajectory of the Cuban novel. In *The Repeating Island,* Benítez Rojo identifies the search for origins, for roots, the need for rediscovery of the divided self, and the cultural fragmentation that originated with the plantation as recurring elements in the Caribbean novel. *Memory Mambo* explores themes common to the Caribbean novel, with equal concern for historical specificity, in this case the historical specificity of Cuban émigrés in the United States. The origins remain the same, but the journey back is longer and more circuitous, since the point of departure for the émigré writer is that of a Caribbean once removed. In the development of Cuban literature, we find that the passage from *lo criollo* to *lo cubano*—from a sense of Caribbeanness to a Caribbean, Cuban nationalism—was, in broad strokes, a movement from Europe to Cuba. The conclusion of Méndez Capote's *Memorias de una cubanita que nació con el siglo* suggests precisely that swing away from Old World origins toward an embrace of Caribbeanness as the European-educated bourgeoisie comes to terms with the extreme limitations of independence as defined by the republic in its second decade. For Méndez Capote and the class she inhabits and represents, facing the present constructively, with an eye to shaping the future, meant letting go of the past, of traditions that were disintegrating, in any case, under U.S. dominance.

If there was a strong sense of unity among the early émigrés (who, once uprooted, had no one to hold onto except each other), by the 1990s that coherence has been severely eroded. The protagonist of *Memory Mambo* is adrift in a disintegrating universe with nothing to rely on but

herself. Surrounded by émigrés who have done nothing but lie to themselves and each other since their arrival, Juani's is a journey into historical truth. Remembering and forgetting, truth and lies, both move the
plot forward and shape the characters' narratives. Juani's discourse rises
to the challenge of not telling lies to herself, though the climax of the
novel revolves around a lie she has presented to the others and must
now retract. The protagonist's truth-seeking and truth-telling narrative
is meant to serve as counterpoint to the false memories expressed in the
collective narrative of the enclave of exile. As narrator, her function is
that of Carpentier's novelistic Adam, naming and renaming the things
of her world, a world in which nothing is solid and all appearances
deceive.

From the first line to the last, *Memory Mambo* describes the form and
content of a disintegrating social reality. The identity of the émigré
community is coming apart at the seams, in the family, the community,
the enclave itself. Survival depends on abandoning the myth of cohesion,
confronting the process of disintegration, and struggling to create something new with the pieces as they fall away. The narrator describes communication among exiles as one that takes place in a vernacular, a way
of speaking, that is "neither Cuban nor American, neither genetic or
processed." In a line that resonates throughout the narrative, the protagonist defines the linguistic and existential terrain negotiated by all
the novel's characters: "We communicate, I suspect, like deaf people—
not so much compensating for the lost sense, but creating a new syntax
from the pieces of our displaced lives." The narrator succeeds while
those around her fail. By rejecting false memory, she is able to regain the
historical continuity others have lost and to reassemble the pieces of her
displaced life, sorting out fact from fiction, from the multifaceted fic-
tions that are shaped and reshaped in a vicious cycle that entraps. In her
reflections on the meaning of memory and search for historical truth,
the narrator begins at the beginning, recounting the facts—what she
has been able to gather of the *who, what, why, when,* and *where*—of her
family's departure from Cuba: "I didn't know what was going on. I was
simply gathered up, like one more precious belonging, and packed into
a stranger's bloated car in the middle of the night, then taken down
through black, rural roads with the car lights turned off. . . . So if these
are the facts, why do I remember so much more?" (*Memory Mambo,* 10).
Too young to have retained memories distinctly her own of these events,
what she "remembers" are the versions disseminated by her father, the
versions she will challenge and eventually dismantle.

Why do I remember driving around senselessly, for days, in and out of beaches outside of La Habana (Guanabo, Cojímar, Mariel, even as far away as San Pedro), combing though tall grasses and dirt, as fascinated by the tiny, translucent frogs on tree branches as by the malevolent shadows scurrying underneath? My father planned our escape this way, but I never went along on these excursions. So why is it I can see my father's body, gleaming like larvae, vanishing into the water just off the shore? It's a fact that he swam along the coast, checking the bottom for coral and traps, testing the *milicianos,* trying to see how far out he could go before they'd notice. It's true that I've heard the stories, but I never went along. I never saw the motions, so how can I remember my father shaking the water off like a dog, the salt drying on his body, the hurried, nervous way he unearthed the street clothes he'd buried in newspapers in the sand? (*Memory Mambo,* 10–11)

In a concerted effort to extirpate false memory, the narrator develops a strategy all her own, a foolproof method for isolating the fragments of her own consciousness by teaching herself to identify the particular slant each family member has put on the narrative of departure she memorized long ago, creating the false consciousness she is now determined to shed, layer by layer. She begins by unraveling her father's version because his brand of distortion is the most readily identifiable: "If these aren't my memories, then whose are they? Certainly not my father's— he always cast himself as the stoic hero in his stories, unshakable and inscrutable. . . . If these were my father's stories, they would be wholly congratulatory and totally void of meaningful detail. . . . My cousin Patricia says that this is because his tales are almost always lies" (*Memory Mambo,* 11).

Part historian, in search of the piece, the fragment, the detail that will shed new light on the whole; part detective, who must listen astutely to all accounts to establish grounds for interpreting past events, Juani understands that there are as many versions of an event as there are witnesses to it. Only by lining up all the versions, placing them side by side to expose their particular distortions, can history begin to be explained: "I don't long for a perfect memory. I don't want to ensnare the universe; I already know that's beyond the flawed connections of my small and curious brain. . . .What I want to know is what *really* happened" (*Memory Mambo,* 14). Thus concludes the first chapter, after which the novel shifts to the present. The quest for "what *really* happened" *is* the novel, as the narrator explores the slippery terrain of memory that informs each character's articulation with the world.

The cast of characters is an extended family of relatives, honorary relatives known as "cousins in exile," and friends, in Chicago, Mexico, New York, and Florida. As they interact in the novel, Obejas establishes a hierarchy based on connectedness to Cuba, to the island itself, its history, its culture, and, most importantly, its present. Those with the closest connections are the least likely to fall into the stasis imposed by false memory. And closeness to those characters, in turn, brings Juani closer to her goal of reconnecting with historical Cuba, the Cuba that exists in real time, not the fictional island of memory, frozen in the past. Caridad, Juani's cousin who is married to Jimmy, Juani's and the novel's principal antagonist, represents the strongest link in the chain that connects island and enclave, because she was formed in the culture of the island's present: "Since she's one of the older cousins, she actually learned to dance in Cuba, where they play the really authentic music—not just Celia Cruz, but Beny Moré, Arsenio Rodríguez, Celeste Mendoza and Los Van Van too—so she got assigned to teach all of us younger cousins how to dance. Patricia's the oldest of all, but she was born in New York, which we joke is the reason she can't dance worth a damn" (*Memory Mambo,* 17–18).

The narrator's startlingly direct recognition of the political shadings that exist within every émigré family goes beyond the almost incidental acknowledgment of admiration, bordering on envy, for Caridad's early immersion in *real* Cuban culture on the island. Her recognition occurs at the very center of the novel, exactly midway in the text, and signals a significant rupture with narratives of nostalgia and the myth of the Cuban-American monolith, the fiction of a seamless unity, that so often accompanies them. As Édouard Glissant observes in the epigraph that opened this chapter, when sameness is the standard, beneath that surface a great diversity is most probably being sublimated or, worse yet, repressed. The myth of the Cuban-American monolith has certainly been challenged in scholarly and journalistic writings of recent years. That Achy Obejas has made its debunking a central theme of her novel constitutes a new development in Cuban-American literature. Where other Cuban-American narratives have skirted the issue of the 1959 revolution that created the contemporary diaspora, alluding to, but rarely grappling with, it directly, Obejas leads each of the characters in *Memory Mambo* to confront it, politically, historically, and culturally. Chapter 10 opens with a framing of Cuban-American reality in terms of diversity and nuance, rather than sameness, signaling a sea change in narrative fiction: "In every Cuban family, there is also—no matter how much it may be denied—at least one person who at one time ardently supported Fidel Castro and the Cuban revolution. My Tío Raúl, Patricia and Manolito's father, was that person in our family" (*Memory Mambo,* 100).

The novel's central chapter tells Tío Raúl's story from multiple angles as the other characters reveal their attitudes toward his earlier revolutionary activities and aspirations. A struggling painter in New York, Raúl is recruited to the cause by Haydée Santamaría, one of its central figures. Raúl participates in the assault on the Moncada barracks and manages to escape into the countryside unscathed and eventually make his way to Costa Rica. Although he is determined to join up with Fidel in Mexico for the next offensive, a string of fortuitous events (cast into the plot by Obejas with delicious irony) prevents Raúl from meeting his goal. Instead, his career as a painter takes off following a one-man show in Soho. The entire show sells out at the opening; he walks away with $20,000 and lives from that day forward as a "rich artist." But this success story, with all its twists and turns, is no Horatio Alger tale. Obejas removes it from the realm of cliché, turning on their heads both the oft-repeated myth of the Cuban people's indomitable entrepreneurial spirit and the myth of the American Dream arrived at through the hard work and thrift of the immigrant. Neither of these myths stands a chance of survival when they become the raw material for Obejas's irreverent critical imagination. Tío Raúl owes his success and wealth not to his own ingenuity but to the influence of Caviancito, a "fortune-telling idiot" and faith healer who had his own radio show in Havana in the Batista years. Caviancito advises Raúl to paint rather than take up again with the revolutionaries and, having done that, advises all of his own relatives to buy Raúl's paintings, predicting that they are destined to increase greatly in value.

Obejas exposes the true story of Tío Raúl's success as one of superstitions, manipulation, and dumb luck. His revolutionary commitment is also revealed, under close examination from numerous angles, to be more a product of vanity and self-aggrandizement than praxis. His daughter Patricia "originally saw her father as an idealistic but weak man who didn't really understand the process of change and revolution." The son's portrait of his father is harshly rigorous, refusing to let a single flicker of opportunism go undetected: "Manolito has another view: Tío Raúl was a *comemierda* during and after the revolution, before and after his art made him rich. Manolito, who works like a mule on a chain with his American father-in-law rehabbing and selling urban properties, hates Raúl's accent in English, his effete ways, and the dumb

luck he has always had with everything, but especially with money"
(*Memory Mambo,* 101). The narrator once more takes up the role of historian, weighing all the versions, not knowing what to believe.

Zenaida, Raúl's wife, becomes an unreflective counterrevolutionary,
an expert at facile rhetoric; Raúl remains a charming opportunist. Their
ensuing separation, like all of the minor and major tragedies contained
within the novel, is the result of a lie that festers: Zenaida's telegram to
Raúl in Mexico in which she claims to have been badly injured in a car
accident that never occurred. He returns to New York, but their union
cannot survive the lie that reunited them.

The end of the marriage is brought on as much by divergent reactions to life in New York as by irreconcilable attitudes toward the Cuban
revolution. Zenaida's disappointment with her lot, in Havana and later
in New York, is transformed by years of passive acceptance of it into an
obsessive fixation on Fidel as the cause of all ills: "She's convinced that
without Fidel her life would have been very different, that perhaps she
and Raúl would have stayed together. Without Fidel, Patricia might not
have ever rebelled, and Manolito might have grown up less hostile and
more secure about his father's love" (*Memory Mambo,* 114). The real roots
of Zenaida's problems, and the cause of her divorce from Raúl, emerge
in New York, where her racist attitudes surface as a result of the couple's
reduced circumstances. Raúl works as a cab driver and dishwasher;
Zenaida, as a maid in a hotel. The impact of the experience is pivotal in
both characters' subsequent development. Whereas contact with racial
and class groups he wouldn't have worked side by side with in Cuba,
coupled with his own run-in with the U.S. brand of institutional racism,
made Raúl an advocate of activist social justice, these experiences made
of Zenaida an embittered reactionary, and a self-denying, confirmed
racist.

> For Tío Raúl, those experiences working side by side with American
> black people were good ones. He listened to new music, like gospel and
> bebop in Harlem, and heard horrible stories about segregation and
> lynchings in the South. Even though New York wasn't officially segre-
> gated, Raúl learned about the invisible color line at the hotel's front door,
> gritted his teeth when landlords told him to his face they didn't rent to
> spiks, and quickly understood that it was his dark skin, not his lack of
> buying power, which prompted sales clerks at retail stores to follow him
> and Tía Zenaida around, relentlessly asking if they needed help. By the
> time Haydée Santamaría came along, Tío Raúl was primed for a battle
> for justice.

> Tía Zenaida reacted differently to their new life. . . . She ate lunch by
> herself, refusing to sit at a table with them for fear that she'd be per-
> ceived as black herself, and wouldn't accept rides from her co-workers
> and their husbands, even if they lived in the same little block in Brook-
> lyn, because she didn't want to be seen getting out of a car with black
> people. (*Memory Mambo*, 103)

In the story of Raúl and Zenaida, Obejas clears the air, dissecting the
social construction of whiteness among the Cuban bourgeoisie and
denouncing it as yet another of the lies that separate, divide, and ultimately conquer the characters.

Earlier in the text, the same scenario is played out between Juani's
own mother and father. Once again, in several key paragraphs, the
entire legacy of positivism and racialist mythmaking in Cuban social
history is laid bare, from the duplicity of Bartolomé de las Casas,
defender of indigenous America yet silent on the slave trade, to the
causes and motives of each party in her parents' union.

> Though my mother is clearly a mixed breed—just touch the *pasitas* on
> her head—and my Abuela Olga is obviously of African descent, my
> mother will do just about anything to deny her real lineage. When she
> saw my father . . . she was sure their kids would be colorless and beau-
> tiful.
>
> Alberto José Casas y Molina wasn't just light skinned though: He
> boasted a splendid ancestry. As we've always been told, we're direct
> descendents of Bartolomé de Las Casas, better known in Cuban lore as
> "The Apostle to the Indies." Las Casas got his name because of his
> alleged work protecting the island's indigenous population from the
> Spaniards' bloodlust.
>
> My mother always professes admiration for Las Casas' humanitarian-
> ism, although, perhaps more importantly, I think she likes the way the
> whole legend around Las Casas positions the question of race between
> white and Indian, consigning most of the issue of blackness to silence.
> (*Memory Mambo*, 32–33)

These three paragraphs contain a thumbnail sketch of the 400 years
of history that have fed her mother's self-negating racism. The narrator
deftly uncovers the actual root causes of her mother's conversion to
counterrevolution. It was not an opposing political philosophy that propelled her into exile, but an early yet certain glimpse of the possibility of
an inclusionary, multiracial democracy that would do away with the
need to "pass" that had for her become a modus vivendi: "When the

revolution triumphed in 1959, nothing stunned my mother more than the fact that that crazy Raúl and his black friends were riding on tanks with Fidel through the city, shooting rounds in the air and getting drunk together. . . . In that instant my mother—who's been struggling to pass her entire life—could see that the order of things had just been altered" (*Memory Mambo,* 35). And she runs from that vision of the possibility of overturning the hierarchies of race, color, and class her entire life, first "to get us out of Cuba, out of Latin America, out of any country where we might couple with anybody even a shade darker than us: We had to go to the United States, which was close by and chock full of frog-eyed white people such as Joe Namath and President Ford" (35).

Like an internal videotape, the mother rewinds to the same frame over and over again to reinforce her racist values and the counterrevolutionary philosophy they justify: "Each time Mami remembers the moment when Raúl, Fidel and his supporters waved and laughed at the multi-colored masses lining the streets of Havana on that historic New Year's Day, she's reborn as a counterrevolutionary" (*Memory Mambo,* 35).

Color, tone, and shading assume multiple meanings in the text, outside the context of race, and the infinite gradations of hair texture and skin tone Juani's family is forever noting and categorizing. Juani's limited memories of Cuba are black-and-white and one-dimensional like the dull family photographs that evoke a landscape she has forgotten. Gina, Juani's Puerto Rican *independentista* socialist lover, has rich, colorful, textured images of Cuba from her many recent trips to the island. She talks eloquently "about Cuba's colors," "how insistent its landscape," the verdant lushness that allowed her finally to understand the Lorca poem "Te quiero verde."

Gina and her freewheeling colleagues believe what their eyes, ears, and consciousness lead them to believe, without the mediation of others. Not constrained by the peculiar family loyalties of the exile community, they follow the political philosophies they have helped to forge, free to shed or modify them as their thought evolves. Juani is not free to do any of these things—to think, explore, gain knowledge of the world on her own terms—until she has reclaimed herself, which she does by the novel's end. It is Gina's firsthand knowledge "not just about Cuba, but about Puerto Rico and everything else," that exacerbates Juani's frustration at her own ignorance, alienation, and inability to effect change. She experiences her existence, the trap of false memory, and the entrapment of family she loves but can neither reconcile with or leave, as a vortex sucking her in like one of the washers she tends at the family laundromat: "Suddenly I hated that I was just sitting there like a big black hole, like the mouth of one of those big industrial washers into which everybody just throws all their dirty clothes" (*Memory Mambo*, 133).

Just as suddenly, in one semiconscious motion, she makes a fist and aims it at Gina's face, breaking bones. The two go at each other until both women are broken and bloody. All the violent episodes in the novel are tied to false memory, repression or denial. One incident invariably breeds another. It is Jimmy, Caridad's physically abusive husband, who invents a cover-up for the lovers, a tale of politically motivated attackers who have pursued Gina because of her ideology. As in the story of Raúl and Zenaida, the cover-up is successful. Everyone accepts it or pretends to accept it, since denial is easier than confronting what may really have happened. Yet trust and love between the two women is broken. The lie endures, but their relationship ends.

The other destructive fiction at the heart of the novel is Juani's father's story of the duct tape formula: "Depending on who's listening to the story, my father says that either he was a prosperous businessman recruited by the CIA after the Cuban revolution (what he told Jimmy, who he knew was anti-Castro), or that he was unemployed and, when the CIA came calling, didn't have any other options (what he told Gina because he didn't want to be provocative). . . . in both versions he certainly believes working for the CIA was a good route into the American business community, where he hoped to market his *cinta magnética*" (*Memory Mambo*, 27). The father's story is preposterous, an outrageously tall tale. His family and a good part of the enclave indulge him in the lie, allowing him to think he invented duct tape, or *cinta magnética*, as he calls it, because they falsely believe this may restore some of his dignity rather than fuel his growing delusions. Through the repetitive retelling of the story, Obejas permits us to study the reactions of the father's interlocutors, establishing a gauge for the characters. The degree of credulity is an exact measure of the degree of alienation from reality, history, and geopolitics. Accordingly, "If Gina had the hardest time, Jimmy had the easiest," bonding with the fallen patriarch over beers and "Nicaraguan cigars grown from Cuban seeds and imported through Mexico" (26).

Gina is the most resistant of the characters to the overwrought tale of conspiracy, in which the CIA steals the father's formula for duct tape in a gesture of ultimate betrayal, worse than that of the Bay of Pigs, because she has her own principles and convictions, based on logic and knowledge of the world. Although Juani struggles against it, it is Gina's unflappable logic that guides Juani out of the vicious cycle and into historical consciousness through a series of confrontations that increase in rigor and terrifying exactitude up to and beyond the point where they come to blows. This is how it begins: "Gina sighed. 'I wouldn't have left.' She paused. 'How about you—if you'd been old enough to decide for yourself—would you have left?' " (*Memory Mambo,* 132). Juani experiences the question as a blow, a stinging provocation, precisely because she had never formulated it for herself, never wondered what she would have done on her own: "And I realized that I'd left Cuba too young to remember anything but snatches of color and scattered words, like the cut-out letters in a ransom note. And what little I could put together had since been forged and painted over by the fervor, malice and nostalgia of others. What did I really know? And who did I believe? Who *could* I believe?" (133).

Although Juani lashes out at Gina, beating her unconscious and thus silencing the voice that raises questions Juani dares not pose for herself, it is Gina who forces Juani to think for herself. The novel's denouement is Juani's odyssey, first thinking her way out of insularity and stasis, then allowing thought, her own independent thinking, to guide her in a series of actions that will take her back to Cuba.

After recuperating in the hospital following the battle with Gina, Juani finds herself at loose ends. She has been replaced at the laundromat; the family no longer needs her to run it. When Patricia, her New York cousin, asks what she will do with herself, Juani responds with an existential proposition: "I know what I want. . . . I was glowing, I could tell. *It was just so right.* . . . I want to go to Cuba" (*Memory Mambo,* 153).

One leg of the journey back to Cuba to reclaim herself entails encountering Miami, where her sister Nena now lives. In Miami, on the way toward the historical connections she seeks, Juani must confront and reject the artificial construction of identity, the house of cards, she has been running from in Chicago. Miami appears to her, on first encounter, even flatter than the Midwest; a new city, "with a kind of stunted look to it," devoid of history. When her sister welcomes her to "Havana, U.S.A.," Juani's rejection of the comparison is immediate and uncompromising: "There's no way Havana's this ugly! . . . Cuba's green and lush and majestic, no matter how badly it may be crumbling. *Te quiero verde,* I remembered" (*Memory Mambo,* 168).

She continues south, to Key West, to "the places where José Martí used to talk to Cuban cigar workers back in the 1800s," and there Juani finds the historical dimension she lacked, the insertion into Cuba's history she needs to begin to sort things out. Back in Miami, at Nena's computer, Juani puts the lie to the duct tape story with information gathered from the Internet, though she still cannot break out of the lie invented for her by Jimmy, the novel's most repressed (and thus most violent) character. It takes another lie to jolt Juani into consciousness, finally letting go of all the lies—her mother's, her father's, Zenaida's—that she has held onto since arriving in this country, and added to with her own. In an explosive, chaotic, and initially implausible scene, Juani witnesses Jimmy's attempt to sexually molest an infant, baby Rosa, her cousin Pauli's child. Believing she is the sole witness, Juani becomes subject to Jimmy's blackmail, according to which one lie will necessarily be traded for another. The story Jimmy invented to conceal what really happened that night between Gina and Juani is to be traded for Juani's silence, her denial of Jimmy's act and acceptance of a new version of events.

Official history requires complicity over and over again in the tangled web of narrative Juani is in the process of unraveling. The price extracted from each accomplice has been high: self-censorship, a slow erosion of the self through repeated silencing of the counternarratives of history, "what *really* happened," and subjugation to the keepers of the official story. Juani was not alone in witnessing Jimmy's attack on the infant; the child's parents saw it as well. And her cousin Patricia, as it turns out, never believed the other official story, the one Jimmy invented after Juani and her lover, Gina, came to blows. Armed with this knowledge, free from the tyranny of the official story, Juani is already on her way back to Cuba, back to a source capable of generating other versions. In the silence that has opened up all around her once the eternal din of the official stories people tell each other stops, at least for her, Juani envisions what her life might have been. The novel's end is the protagonist's beginning. In the quiet all around her, she will begin to tell her own stories: "As we get up to leave, I flick my finger at the fly, freeing it from the puddle of water. It crawls a bit, then takes off, making an aimless loop in the air, then smashes itself against the window pane. . . . It's quiet now" (*Memory Mambo*, 237).

Isolation

Rafael Yglesias's recent novel *Dr. Neruda's Cure for Evil* (1996) opens on a similar note, with a cast of characters Cuban, Cuban-American, and American, of refreshingly diverse political stripes. Early chapters, in memoir form, begin to tell the story of another set of exiles, the labor migrants of the nineteenth century who set out from Spain for Cuba in search of work, and from there to Tampa; the settlers of Ybor City, "not the exiles who now dominate the Cuban-American community."[9] It is 1960, and the narrator's father, a Spanish journalist, is in Cuba preparing a book on the revolution. His reportage has earned him praise in New York and threats in Miami. But the plot takes a turn very early on, leaving the thread of Cuban history and politics behind, focusing instead on contemporary corporate America in the crafting of a psychological drama.

Celebrated contemporary novelist Oscar Hijuelos has taken a similar detour in his literary trajectory. From his first and most Cuban novel, *Our House in the Last World,* to his more recent, *Mr. Ives' Christmas* (1995), Cuba recedes further and further from consciousness and the cultural process of the narrators. Although not a narrator of evocation and nostalgia, celebrating and recreating in his oeuvre *la Cuba de ayer* (the Cuba of bygone days), Hijuelos's narratives recognize Cuba as the distant incubator of an immigrant lineage. Cuba is the historical site of the immigrant roots of a native New Yorker, and the transformation from Cuban to American in one generation is abrupt and final. I find Gustavo Pérez Firmat's work *Life on the Hyphen: The Cuban-American Way,* though far-reaching and controversial, extremely astute in its categorization of degrees of *cubanía* among contemporary Cuban-American writers. Interspersed between essays on pop culture icons such as Gloria Estefan and Desi Arnaz are some deeply thoughtful meditations on the cultural, geographic, and historical trajectory of contemporary Cuban-American writers such as Oscar Hijuelos, Roberto G. Fernández, José Kozer, Virgil Suárez, and Cristina García. Pérez Firmat describes the axis on which Hijuelos's fictional universe turns as being one that moves inexorably away from Cuba and toward the United States, this movement being "the leavetaking of someone who has no choice but to say good-bye."[10] The distance between his native New York and the land of his immigrant family is so great that, as Pérez Firmat observes, "In Hijuelos's fiction Cuba is unreachable" (Pérez Firmat 1994, 136).

According to Pérez Firmat's analysis of language, text, and context, Cuban-American writing can move in either of two directions, toward or away from Cuba. These two extremes are for him represented by novelist Hijuelos and poet José Kozer: "If Oscar Hijuelos composes valedictories to Cuba, José Kozer writes so as not to say goodbye. If Hijuelos writes 'from' Cuba but 'toward' the United States, Kozer writes 'from' the United States but 'toward' Cuba" (Pérez Firmat 1994, 156). Pérez Firmat's "directional" sense of the spirit and letter of contemporary Cuban-American writing is theoretically valid and useful for understanding the vast, differentiated world of off-island writers, and for looking at the dialectical relationship between canon and diaspora. Those who write "from" Spanish into English, and "from" the United States "toward" Cuba, have a much stronger grounding in, or relationship to, the Cuban literary tradition, whereas the writers who belong on the axis that moves from Cuba toward the United States are claiming their place "among American 'ethnic' writers." Pérez Firmat goes on to distinguish between Cuban-Americans who, even if they wrote in English, wrote for other Cuban-Americans, and new generations of writers whose audience may include Cuban-Americans but also transcends the community: "Only in the last couple of years, with the appearance of novels by Hijuelos, Virgil Suárez, and Cristina García, have Cuban-American authors sought to reach a broader audience. The language of these recent novels is strikingly different from that of earlier texts" (144).

García's *Dreaming in Cuban,* a novel of three generations of Cuban women who span geography, history, and political responses to revolution on the island, posits identity as *dream.* The granddaughter Pilar dreams of, and imagines conversations with, her grandmother Celia, the young woman's symbolic connection to a legacy that she feels slipping away from her: "Most days Cuba is kind of dead to me. But every once in a while a wave of longing will hit me and it's all I can do not to hijack a plane to Havana or something. I resent the hell out of the politicians and the generals who force events on us that structure our lives, that dictate the memories we'll have when we're old. Every day Cuba fades a little more inside me, my grandmother fades a little more inside me. And there's only my imagination where our history should be."[11]

In an interview, García made clear that a return trip to Cuba, a reconnection with the culture and context she abandoned as a small child, was a necessary prerequisite for writing the novel. Her statement suggests that only by reinscribing herself, however briefly, in the social landscape of the island could she avoid the Machiavellian dichotomies and generalities that hold in the United States, nurtured by its isolation from Cuba: "There was no sense of formality, no barriers whatsoever. . . . And then I began to hear their stories. They would come out slowly one by one; and a lot from my grandmother in particular. It was during this trip that I got a larger sociopolitical context for being

Cuban. For me, Cuba had been a black and white situation up to that point."[12]

Although the protagonist succeeds in her pilgrimage of return, the novel's end would seem to reconfirm the essential Americanness of her life. In a chaotic Havana, during the weeks that witnessed the flooding of the Peruvian Embassy with would-be émigrés, key characters begin to fall, one by one, into oblivion. In a Santería ritual, her aunt Felicia loses consciousness, "falling into an emptiness without history or future" (*Dreaming,* 187), and the grandmother, Celia, "steps into the ocean and imagines she's a soldier on a mission—for the moon, or the palms, or El Líder" (243). The novel's parting image is one of a consciousness letting go and fading into oblivion. The grandmother, now submerged, removes her pearl earring, "closes her eyes and imagines it drifting as a firefly through the darkened seas, imagines it slowly extinguishing" (244).

The grandmother who remained firmly on the island, with no thoughts of leaving, is the Brooklyn-bound granddaughter's only remaining link to Cuba. With her extinction, the last ties would appear to be severed, casting her adrift, like the pearl on the waves. All that remains where history should be is "imagination" and "dream." In this regard, the novel posits a movement *toward* the United States. The dilemma of cultural identity and self-representation resolves itself in favor of the United States. With no remaining anchors, Cuban identity is cast adrift, with the airy impermanence of the dream that gives the narrative its title.

Identity is posited ambiguously, as dream, in García's narrative. In Hijuelos's *Our House in the Last World,* Cuba is a pathology. The term *microbio* appears repeatedly throughout the coming-of-age tale, suggesting that Cuba is also an illness, physical and mental, that must be fought off if one is to become whole and well. Pérez Firmat, in his interpretation of the novel, takes this assumption to its ultimate conclusions, observing that Héctor, the American-born protagonist, finds release in an English "that bolts the barrio," and for whom "Spanish is the enemy, and the desire is to keep Cuba at a distance—its inflections no less than its infections" (Pérez Firmat 1994, 145).

As opposed to the theories of Cubanness as something that must be worked out of the system, Virgil Suárez, like Achy Obejas, posits Cubanness as a source of strength and renewal, a tonic against alienation. Of the same literary generation as Obejas, Suárez began publishing his fiction in the 1990s, a time when commonly held notions of

Cuban-American identity began to be questioned. His short stories, *Welcome to the Oasis* (1992), and "Settlements," appearing in *Iguana Dreams: New Latino Fiction* (1992), express the existential viewpoint of a generation marked by disillusionment, disaffection, and ennui. Suárez chose as the epigraph for *Welcome to the Oasis* a line from Neruda that perfectly captures that sense of ennui: "Sucede que me canso de ser hombre" [I happen to be tired of being a man]. In Suárez's work, the sense of ennui also reflects the specific malaise of a generation not wearied by the weight of their humanity but simply tired of being Cuban-American. In the title story, "Welcome to the Oasis," a Marielito finds all the ills of prerevolutionary Cuba, the race and class prejudice, reproduced in Miami, so he heads for California. True to the sociological studies that have tracked Mariel émigrés, in California, too, he ends up working for a Cuban. Employed as a housepainter and handyman by Quiroga, an established immigrant who owns a string of apartment-hotels, the Marielito observes the pecking order of Quiroga's subordinates. Within the bleak, self-contained world of the Oasis apartments, each member of the hierarchy takes advantage of the one below him or her. The painter-narrator observes all and tries to remain detached and impartial until a mutiny occurs. The narrator steps in to prevent Quiroga from drowning his own mistress as he repeatedly slaps her at the edge of the pool. He and Quiroga end up in the pool. At the narrative's conclusion, the protagonist is definitely sinking, but he no longer knows if it is his adversary pushing him under or the even greater but less identifiable force of the life the protagonist has come to live: "He is swallowing a lot of water. After a while he can't tell if Quiroga's hands are still holding him down. Something's certainly pulling the painter down, down, and it feels like it's never going to let go."[13]

"Settlements" is the tale of a young painter who drifts from Los Angeles to Tucson, not so much heading toward something as away from L.A., hoping that a change of scenery will inspire his canvases, which seem to be "going nowhere." In Tucson, he drifts into a relationship with a young woman from whom he rents part of a house. In the Tucson landscape, his paintings improve, but the relationship goes nowhere. The narrative is circular in structure. As the story begins, the aimless young man tells his father that he is taking to the road to prove to his mother that he is actually headed somewhere:

> "I want to prove to her that I'm headed in the right direction."
> "What direction's that, son?"

"Southeast," I said, "I want to go to the desert. Fill up the gas tank
and ride, ride, ride."[14]

At the story's end, still adrift, the aimless narrator returns, having
gained nothing from his sojourn in the Southeast: "I returned to L.A. to
deal with old ghosts and to prove to everyone I knew what I was doing"
("Settlements," 309).

The fairly anonymous protagonist of "Settlements" assumes a
sharper, more complex identity in the novel *Going Under*, for which the
short story provides the germ. Here, the vaguely Hispanic painter
becomes a YUCA, a young, upwardly mobile Cuban-American, and
acquires a history. The novel's plot unfolds in the heyday of furious yuppie-
dom that now seems like a distant memory, and it is set "in Miami during the Last Days of the Reagan years." To make the reference to the
greed of the Reagan years that threatens to claim the protagonist's soul
even clearer, Suárez includes an Abakuá proverb that means "avarice
corrupts."

The novel opens with an image of pointless modernity, stagnation,
and the ultimate status symbol of a yuppie's version of the American
Dream: Xavier Cuevas, stuck in traffic in his 240 GL Volvo, on the
Miami expressway at rush hour. He is going nowhere, "going under,"
and the only way to reverse the process is to go *home*. Like Juani Casas of
Memory Mambo, Xavier flees Miami, headed for Key West, the southern-
most point in the United States and the closest to Cuba, to reconnect
with and reclaim a fading heritage. The novel's closing image is of
Xavier diving into the ocean and swimming home.

Between those two images of the lost and the found, Suárez constructs a taut existential novel as astute in its critique of a mainstream
America that has lost its compass as it is of the Cuban-American middle
class, which, in striving to be all-American and all-Cuban, all things to
all people, ends up *anonadada,* that is, a rootless people in a no-man's-
land, neither Cuban nor American.

Suárez's novel unfolds in sparse, penetrating language. We follow
Xavier Cuevas through the days of deal making at the insurance agency
he owns, and the long, stressful nights he spends awake watching his
children and American wife, Sarah, sleep. When he does sleep, it is a
restless sleep punctuated by anxiety-fueled nightmares.

Skillfully recreating the endless striving of what came to be known as
the "go-go" eighties, Suárez fills the text with all the symbols of that
period transposed to Miami—the imposing house in Coral Gables, cars

and clubs Xavier cannot really afford—yet never allows the descriptions to fall into the realm of the commonplace or to become elements in a morality play. There is a mounting tension underlying all of Xavier's actions until his vision and life itself become painful. As his awareness of his own alienation grows keener, Xavier begins to feel out of sorts, physically ill, while those around him remain unaffected. The very condition of being Cuban-American is defined in the novel as a slow process of "going under," shared by all the characters, whether they are conscious of it or not. If exile is "false memory" for Achy Obejas, Suárez portrays it as a purgatory inhabited by those who wait eternally for something that will never happen, like the annual toast to "next year in Havana." Suárez's characters are all stuck; they have become Cuban-American and forgotten how to be Cuban in the decades of waiting through an ill-defined existence, holding out for the moment of return to become themselves again. Suárez's Cuban-American characters, like Samuel Beckett's who wait for Godot, have a surreal cast to them; at once frenetic and static, they wear themselves out while running in place. The protagonist allows himself to sink into the quagmire with all the others, but unlike the others, he finds that the nullity of his daily existence is killing him, literally. Xavier continues to fall into the abyss until he is nearly comatose as the result of a self so divided it has become unhinged. Although he suffers from high blood pressure and stress-related illness, it is to a *santera* that Xavier goes in search of a cure. She locates his "illness" not in his arteries but in the zone of his identity.

> "What do you want to know?"
> "*Todo,* everything."
> Reluctant at first, Xavier spoke slowly, filling in gaps of conversation with silence, then not so self-conscious anymore, he told Caledonia everything he could about his aspirations of one day making a lot of money in the insurance business, but yet all that had been undermined by a strong feeling of detachment and dislocation. Insecurities plagued him, so he no longer knew what he wanted to do, or whether what he was doing meant anything. Things, as they happened fast, were falling apart.
> "Are you Cuban or American?" she asked.
> "I feel more American than I do Cuban."
> "But you're not Cuban. That is, you don't *feel* Cuban."
> Xavier nodded.[15]

The protagonist chooses a *santera* over a psychologist or a psychiatrist to help him out of his troubles because the latter would oblige him to talk about his past, and "the last thing Xavier wanted to do was think about his past when he no longer felt he had one" (*Going Under,* 85). It is not precisely the sensation that he has no past that is tormenting Xavier Cuevas, but rather that he has the wrong past because he has been "living the wrong life." He comes to the conclusion that he is not Cuban enough, and not by accident of circumstance but by choice. He has lost himself and is responsible for his own destiny. The *cubanía* posited by Suárez is an active and activist claiming of history, not an accident of birth. Suárez thus negates the hand-me-down version of Cuban identity among the diaspora by restating its essence as existential choice. Similarly, in his version of Cuban Miami and Hialeah, it is not the predominance of the culture of the enclave that comes across but rather its diluted quality, its distance from the source. It is, once again, the haunting feeling of a diluted Cubanness, a rupture with tradition, that feeds his discontent, whereas the Cuban-Americans around him perceive only a saturation of "ethnic" culture. Cuba tugs at him, but it is not a longing for the company of relatives left behind that draws him but the more substantive pull of history and tradition.

The other force fueling Xavier's crisis is the poverty of the American culture that surrounds him, the only culture to which he can lay claim. Whatever had once appeared solid in American life is falling away, causing him to question everything. The experience of watching late-night television is "as close as he'd ever come to turning himself off," and he attributes television's popularity to its narcotic, numbing effect: "After Johnny Carson and David Letterman, after the news on CNN and Headline News, after the animal shows on the Discovery Channel, after all the stupid and nonsensical music videos on MTV and VH1, after the true-to-life crime and cop shows, after the black and white movie on the Classics Channel, after the reruns of shows he'd watched as a kid, after all that, America lost its soul" (*Going Under,* 140).

American culture is numbing, and Cuban-American culture is the ultimate alienation. The realization that he is caught between these two poles, one worse than the other, precipitates the narrator's crisis, allowing him, in turn, to envision a way out of the vicious circle. Xavier's crisis is brought on not by partial assimilation but rather by excessive assimilation. Successful assimilation appears in the text as a form of toxicity. For Héctor, the protagonist of Hijuelos's *Our House in the Last World,* the remaining unassimilated elements of Cubanness are the root cause of his malaise, the obstacles to wholeness in the journey away from Cuba and into America. For Xavier, the one undiluted drop of Cubanness remaining in his aggressively assimilated persona will ultimately serve as antidote to the "illness" of contemporary America: "At school no one ever made fun of him because he didn't look like an outsider. An immigrant. A wetback. He fit in and so the children left him alone. That was the beginning of a transition in the unbalance of identity. More American, less Cuban. He was second generation. For all practical purposes, he got by, and that was the problem. . . . This was his place. His country. He'd been here ninety-nine percent of his life; but the one percent couldn't be ignored. Obviously, that one percent made all the difference" (*Going Under*, 138).

En route to Key West, he has a confrontation with the chimera of San Lázaro, a blind old man in rags at a roadside bar, who chides Xavier for having lost his center, for not knowing how to be Cuban, no matter where he is. From that point on, the narrator's strategy of resistance and survival is to cultivate "that one percent" and, through it, to learn how to be Cuban again.

Xavier Cuevas has been "going under" throughout the course of the novel, throughout the course of a lifetime. When he falls into an actual coma midway through the novel, the physical crisis jolts him into the realization that, spiritually, he has been functioning as if comatose all of his life. The final scene is a different sort of "going under," this time with his eyes wide open, "swimming home." The text is open-ended; it presumes no final destiny for the protagonist. What matters is the journey; undertaking that journey symbolizes an active embrace of historicity and heritage. Without that, there can be nothing, no possible point of departure:

> *Why can't I be Cuban here?*
> *Because geography matters. Geography and climate matter. This is what I'm talking about. You've lost your way because you've become a bland mix of nothing but routines. Thoughtless, meaningless routines. . . .*
> *So what's the answer?*
> *Go back . . . go back to where you belong, your rightful place in time. Our history, your history, is one of returning.* (*Going Under*, 119)

Roberto G. Fernández's *La vida es un special, .75* provides a response to the question raised by Suárez's protagonist. In Fernández's wild and wildly innovative collage of a novel, the whole range of tragicomic characters illustrate graphically, with their disjuncture and distortions, why no one can be Cuban in Miami. As an editor's preface to the author's own prologue explains, Fernández offers "a narrative of the new Cuban

folklore born in exile. The confusion of two cultures (and three, four
. . .), of bilingualism and the birth of a new sociological case, that of
Miami; all of this is reflected in the text."[16] The novel is a kaleidoscope
of fragments that the reader may assemble and reassemble at will, narrated by a wide cast of characters, in which Fernández recreates the
microcosmos miamense. The different tones and registers employed in the
text, in English, Spanish, and a hybrid of the two, reflect generational
difference and conflict. Language also reflects the degree of assimilation
into, or alienation from, the Cuban enclave of Miami, as in the episode
titled "Micky," in which an older, non-English-speaking Cuban encounters Micky on the bus. The older Cuban, who needs information from
the bus driver, is confident that the young man will serve as a translator,
but what transpires instead is absolute miscommunication, ending with
Micky's utter, willful rejection of both the Spanish language and the
neighbor. Micky desires nothing but escape—escape into English and
his anglicized nickname.

> Pero bueno, gracias al cielo que me he topado contigo.
> —What?
> —Sí, ¡ ha sido la gran casualidad!
> —Excuse me, I can't understand you.
> —¿Tú no eres el hijo de Serafina?
> —I'm sorry but I can't understand you.
> —Claro que si onderstand mi, si yo he oído cuando tu madre te grita:
> M-I-G-U-E-L-I-T-O M-A-I-Q-U-I a comer.
> —Please, I don't want to understand you.
> —Sí. Tú mismo eres Miguelito Hernández, el hijo de Serafina.
> —My name is Micky. I don't understand you. (*La vida*, 49)

In the novel's early pages, we are introduced to Eloy de los Reyes, the
text's and the community's "bargain-basement" archaeologist, as he
attempts to rediscover his Cuban origins by transforming his bathroom
into an ersatz Varadero Beach, and recreating the landscape of his native
Oriente in another room. He gets stuck early in the process of reinsert-
ing himself within Cuba's history, as all the characters who attempt it
inevitably do. Rising at dawn, he fills the room with coconuts, pineapples, mangoes, and avocados, fashions six feathers into a headdress,
and begins to hum an homage to Oriente, birthplace of the Siboney
Indians: "Caney de Oriente tierra de amores / cuna florida donde nació
el siboney / donde las frutas son . . . son . . . / donde las frutas son . . .
son . . ." (*La vida*, 14).

Unable to recall any of the fruits that grow in Oriente, he gives up and drifts off, on to something else. The reader has by now realized that the self-proclaimed archaeologist, keeper of Cuba's past in exile, has no knowledge of the historical past himself and is thus incapable of the task he has set himself.

Later in the text, in a continuation of Eloy's pursuit of Cuba's pre-Columbian history, a series of *areitos,* the ceremonial gatherings of the *siboneyes* and *taínos,* is reenacted. It is in the Areito series—Areitos I through IV—that Fernández's ironic treatment of the characters' absolute ignorance of Caribbean history surpasses mere pathos and enters the realm of the surreal.

In the first Areito, archaeologist Eloy attempts to reconstruct the games played during the indigenous ceremony. His only affirmative sentences are grossly reductionist generalities used to differentiate between *taínos, siboneyes,* and *caribes;* between these are the gaping lacunae he fills with elements taken from contemporary U.S. culture.

> The participants in the *areito* were naked, although the women covered their sex with a tuft of cotton. The nicest ones were the Siboneys. The Tainos were good too. But not as noble. The Tainos were more advanced. I'm sure they were the ones who invented the game with the circle and the ball. Once in a while, the Caribs came. They were very cruel. But they weren't from there. They came from somewhere else. So, in reality, all I need is a ball, then everyone forms a circle, a group of naked people, except the women who cover themselves with a piece of cotton, and finally, some mute dogs. I think we could also use a bat. The Tainos must certainly have used a bat . . . (*La vida,* 33; translation mine)

Subsequent versions presented in Areitos II, III, and IV reflect the younger generation's even greater lack of knowledge of colonial and twentieth-century Cuba, as well as that of contemporary Florida. Like Eloy, his young interlocutors fill in the enormous gaps in their grasp of history with whatever pops into their heads, creating, as they go along, a new and wacky mythology, unique to the Miami enclave. In Areito II, nostalgia for a recent, prerevolutionary past (which this generation has only heard about from parents and grandparents) is grafted onto elements of the elders' distorted version of the pre-Columbian history of the Caribbean.

> —¿Qué les parece si celebramos el areito el 7 de diciembre?
> —Es el día del attack a Pearl Harbor.

—Bueno sí, pero esa fecha tiene que ver con otra cosa más que ahora no recuerdo exactamente.

—Anyway, what's un areito?

—Es una celebración de los siboneyes y los taínos. Jugaban a la pelota, tenían perros mudos y las mujeres . . .

—That's funny. Mi abuela never talks de un areito. But she had many criadas. Y tenía una finca muy grande that almost reached the sea. Sometimes, iban a la capital en un private train. Now, mi abuelo was really something else. He was cool. Tenía un yate y un private driver. Los summers se los pasaba en un private key. But they never talk about un areito. Are you sure is not a tropical fruit? (*La vida,* 33–34)

The construction of an unlikely mythology from a basis of absolute ignorance—the longing for a past that no one cares enough about to study—is a central theme that runs through the text, across the collage of voices. Another is an exploration of the ideology of "freedom," produced and reproduced among the exiles, against the backdrop of their relentless and simultaneous pursuit of bargains; the desire to get something for nothing, or almost nothing. And it is this theme that generates the work's most profoundly ironic juxtapositions. In one scene, a radio crew in a mobile unit heads downtown to broadcast the live interview of the day. The radio personalities find and select for the spot a very recent Cuban immigrant but are unwilling to let him speak for himself. Instead, they interrupt his every word with their own purple prose paeans to liberty, Miami style.

—Tell me, how long have you been here?

—Two weeks.

—How were things there when you left?

—Well . . .

—Tell me, why did you decide to leave?

—Well, I had a cousin here and . . .

—No doubt it was your longing for freedom that brought you to these shores.

—Well, I had a cousin here and I. . .

—You fulfilled that longing that you longed for two weeks ago and I can see that you've taken on new colors breathing the air of freedom.

—Well, you see, I had a cousin here and I told her that if one day. . .

—He who has suffered the lack of freedom, dear listeners, today can breathe, feel free, and sing the praises of freedom. (*La vida,* 49–50; translation mine)

In what they trust will be a gloriously clichéd conclusion to the interview of the day, the reporters give the man the microphone, and the last word. He responds with a countercliché, a materialist vision of hunks of ham, and the two opposing clichés form an impenetrable duet, one that closes in on itself, since neither interviewers or interviewee will admit any deviation from the format of their own obsession:

> —And what else would you like to tell the radio audience?
> —Well, you see, I had a cousin here and I told her that if one day. Well, señor, to be honest, I came to eat ham. Yes, that's it, and I would like to declare to the public that I have always liked grilled ham a lot. And that's why I came.
> —And freedom is important too? Isn't it?
> —Yes, that's important, and so is grilled ham. (*La vida,* 50; translation mine)

In a satiric fragment titled "Varadero Gran Finale," identity and *cubanía* are posited as dream, a state attainable only through the workings of the unconscious mind. Devoid of sentimentality, the dream becomes a neurotic, alienated nightmare, "una porquería desbalanceada" [an unstable bunch of crap] (*La vida,* 87; translation mine). In the dream of Varadero, instead of sand and ocean there are willows and blue mountains, castles and swans, and no doubt or uncertainty, until everything suddenly falls apart: "And honey rained down from the sky, and everyone came to the castle to consult with the king and no one had uncertainties because the king resolved them all, but suddenly, a man appeared and prevented you from building a castle, telling you to read the sign, that it wasn't allowed, and with one kick he wrecked your kingdom, and the lake emptied of water, and the swans flew away, and the willows dried up" (87; translation mine). In the parable, as in all the episodes in Fernández's Cuban-American tapestry, the recompense for the collapse of past glories, real or imagined, is easy to come by and always close at hand in Miami: a special, a bargain, a bit of contraband: "That's why I always go to your *areitos*; I visit you in Varadero and tell you where they have coconuts, pineapples and mangoes on special, and if I find contraband mamey, I bring you some" (87; translation mine).

In Fernández's intelligent, irreverent, original novel, bilingualism is less a linguistic condition than the reflection of a state of mind, often the exteriorization of inner confusion, imbalance, lack of control. Spanish and English cohabit uneasily in Fernández's Miami, where Cuba is a mythology, and English a betrayal. It is the odd and exclusive limbo of the Cuban enclave that Fernández captures in his fiction; his characters inhabit a world unto themselves. The English and the Spanish that the characters speak are peppered with references to a Cuban exile mythology that makes both languages practically incomprehensible outside the frame of reference of the enclave. Fernández holds the rigorous, historical mirror of critical distance up to the distorted reality of the enclave and allows it to be seen clearly. As Pérez Firmat noted in *Life on the Hyphen,* Fernández's characters speak "an inspired gibberish"; the elements of his literary collage are "hilarious recastings" in which "everything and nothing is lost in translation" (Pérez Firmat 1994, 144).

Estrangement, disjuncture, and the pull of two cultures, two ways of life, are also at the heart of Marisella Veiga's haunting existential tale of two island women. "Fresh Fruit" is a small gem of narrative. In less than three pages, and with a verbal economy that rivals that of Horacio Quiroga, master of the short story genre in Latin America, Veiga is as eloquent in what she leaves unsaid as in what her narrative reveals.

On an unnamed Antillean island, two women observe each other's lives. Although the narrative unfolds in real time, from daybreak to sundown, on one day, or one of any number of identical days, there are flashbacks to the past and projections into the future that provide a telescoping of time. Everything we come to know of the two women is revealed in the details, details that seem to branch out, to expand and encompass the full social and cultural dimensions of their lives. Through the accumulation of details and nuance, we come to know who each woman is, where she has come from, and where she is going.

The dominant voice and vision is that of the older woman, whose daily morning routine opens the narrative:

> I was up the first time about five, made coffee and heated up some milk for it. When I turned on the kitchen light, the dog came and stood near the stove. He seemed cold. Right before lunch I usually boil some meat and bones for him, but it was not time for that feeding, so I gave him a little warm milk instead. I snapped the light off and went to sit on the porch, where I usually have my coffee and listen to the roosters and the occasional car traveling along the highway.[17]

The older woman's world projects inward; her life is one of service (to husband, neighbors, and dog), quietude, and the regret she transforms into the judgmental conformism that she projects onto the young woman who lives across the street. The older woman's life is inscribed within a silence that is punctuated by her husband's arrivals and departures at precisely timed intervals. The young neighbor's life, in contrast, projects outward, from the home to the world, and is characterized by movement and the noises that accompany it: the clank of a gate as she leaves for work in the morning, the roar of a car's engine as she starts it up, the greeting she yells from across the street when she returns in the evening. The older woman remains fixed, inside looking out, or on the porch, facing the street, and thus has the greater opportunity to observe. Her observations, however, are colored by her own condition, and we must distrust her conclusions about the younger woman's life: "She started that old car with tremendous faith. It's as loud as a motorcycle. Sometimes, as the car warms up, she looks over to see if I am on the porch and waves. In the morning she is relaxed, friendlier. By late afternoon she is tired and a bit arrogant, thinking that what she does all day is more important than what I do. I can tell by the excuses she makes when I call her to come over for a short visit" ("Fresh Fruit," 351).

By turns envious and resentful of the younger woman's autonomy, the narrator compares her unwillingness to linger, the abruptness of her comings and goings, with the conduct of her own husband. When the narrator silences the internal censor and simply watches, records, and reflects on the younger woman's actions, her observations are pithy, acute, and revealing, as in a passage on the political economy of the world of unmarried professionals: "Susana, of course, has the option to not make anyone anything. Every morning at the corner cafeteria she reads a newspaper while having breakfast. Someone cooks it and somebody else takes the dishes away when the meal is done. She does not even see the faces of the people performing these services. Throwing away money, that's all. I told her she could pay me less and have more delicious food, but I don't think she's interested in saving money either, or forming a home with a husband" ("Fresh Fruit," 352). That which is left unsaid here is, of course, that Susana's conduct is censurable to the observer because she is female. If she were a young man, the money and labor of others spent so that she may feed herself would be of no consequence and thus go unnoticed and unrecorded.

The story's title is tersely and beautifully evoked in a poetic passage on age, the promise of youth and the passage of time. In it, the older woman lets slip that she was once like Susana, or would like to have been: "No sweets. Give her the sea, the beginning of the meal and she's happy. I know. Now I want the sweet, the fruit the comes after the meal is done" ("Fresh Fruit," 353).

By the story's conclusion, we have become aware, in stages, that it is among other things an exploration of solitude; two distinct forms of solitude, their contours and dimensions: the solitude of a woman come of age within a traditional Antillean marriage, with security but without camaraderie, and the solitude of a young single professional woman, with "American ways, which she learned at school." Because the entire narrative is told from the married woman's perspective, cast from within her worldview, we never discover whether the younger woman is content with the life she is shaping for herself. It does not matter; the ambiguity heightens the narrative's quiet tension. What matters is the older woman's examination of her own life as a result of her proximity to, and interest in, Susana's life, a life the narrator has not and, given her generation, could not have lived: "Yes, she is free to wander beyond her gate, to walk into a restaurant any time of day, like any man, and buy meals made by someone cooking anonymously in the kitchen. She has money, a way to ride around town. She speaks English and French and travels to the other islands. She drinks beer and sometimes stays out late, while I sit on my porch waiting for Wilfredo to arrive. I don't get bored" ("Fresh Fruit," 353).

Veiga does not tip the scales for us; she merely holds up the two women's lives for us to ponder. She carefully controls the narrative's flow to reveal only the observer's contradictory philosophy of food, nourishment, and life, a philosophy shaped by fulfillment and longing, self-satisfaction and envy, a sense of her own powerlessness and a pride in the discreet, manipulative power held by the woman "behind the throne": "When Wilfredo and I were first married, we rented a small apartment in this neighborhood, near the sea, and spent Sundays on the beach. Years later, he bought this house and a few years after that a farm in the mountains, so our home would not lack fresh fruit or vegetables. I haven't seen the farm in years; I don't leave the house, but he drives up there often and returns with the back of his jeep loaded with bunches of plantains" ("Fresh Fruit," 352).

The tale of the two women's lives concludes with a glimpse into the interior of the two houses, one on either side of the street, at day's end; one abandoned, the other inhabited. Veiga, thus, focuses at close range on the conditions of the two women, their distinct relationships to the home and the world:

> Her house is empty all day until she walks into it. She can stroll along the shore of the sea anytime, but there, nobody gives a damn. There she

goes, out to dinner again, taking a book along for company. I'll start frying up plantains. Wilfredo will be home in an hour.

After the meal and some conversation, he will turn off the lights in the dining room. I'll wash the dishes and close up the kitchen, and finally bring the dog inside the house for the night. We will go through the rest of the rooms, turning off the lights in the entire house, before going our separate ways. ("Fresh Fruit," 353)

The starkness of the prose intrigues. With few adjectives and little physical description of place, the two women's lives might seem to unfold almost anywhere. But the accumulation of small, significant detail belies the apparent universality of the tale's setting. We are most definitely on an island, albeit unidentified, and these are distinctly pan-Antillean women. The context and texture of their lives reflects the condition of contemporary women across the generational divide whether in Puerto Rico, Cuba, or the Dominican Republic. From the opening lines on, Veiga has subtly situated us in the Antilles with the heating of milk for *café con leche,* the sound of roosters crowing near a highway, the salty *tostones* the younger woman prepares for herself from the plantains the other woman's husband brings back from the mountains. But it is Susana who is clearly the pan-Caribbean figure, armed with Spanish, French, and English, languages that, combined with her travels, permit and establish her connection to the other islands of the Caribbean.

Chapter Four

From Lost Steps to Hyphenated Lives: Cuban Voices and Latino Literature

If Fernández Retamar revised and updated such essays as "Our America and the West" and "Caliban Revisited," he would no doubt grapple with migrations of intellectuals whose condition is not that of exile, but of hybridity and between-ness. His work in the 1990s, along with that of many postcolonial intellectuals, sees his productions as inescapably political, always "written for" alliances in our global Borderlands.

—José David Saldívar, *The Dialectics of Our America* (1991)

The journey from the mid–twentieth century to the 1990s marks for the Americas a movement away from the paradigm of analysis that governed virtually all thinking on Latin America for the last 50 years. There is undeniably no turning back from the current process of fragmentation and reorganization on a global scale, raising critical questions about its cultural and social consequences. The Latin American dependency theorists of the late 1960s and early 1970s stood the debate about development on its head, redefining the terms, rules, and even the name of the game, by taking Latin America as the starting point for devising alternative strategies. Cuban poet and literary theorist Roberto Fernández Retamar's *Calibán: Apuntes sobre la cultura de nuestra América* emerged in that period and was shaped by it conceptually. In that work, Retamar challenged the Latin American intelligentsia to adopt a new optic, to examine the historical development of Latin American literature, culture, and the arts from the perspective of Caliban, the subjugated yet indomitable figure of Shakespeare's *The Tempest* who represents the unbroken thread of indigenous resistance to colonization. Retamar's essay is, in turn, a rethinking of José Martí's 1896 cultural manifesto for Latin America "Nuestra América." Both thinkers sought to articulate from a uniquely Cuban perspective the process of identity formation at turning points in Latin American history. In defining Latin America from "the inside out," Martí was reacting to the threat of absorption by the United States, and Retamar to the isolation of Cuba as a result of increasing international polarization. Retamar reflects on those times in "Caliban Revisited," asking readers to recall their bitterness: "My piece was not born in a vacuum but rather at a particular time that was marked by passion, and—on our part—indignation at the paternalism, the rash accusation against Cuba, and even the grotesque 'shame' and 'anger' of those who, comfortably situated in the 'West' with their fears, their guilt, and their prejudices, decided to proclaim themselves judges of the revolution."[1] The Cold War had imposed and refined the categories of "us" and "them" to which Retamar was reacting by proclaiming the right of a Latin American "we" to define itself, on its own terms, in a manifesto that shaped the thinking of a generation.

Carpentier's Latin American–born, New York–based protagonist of the 1953 novel *The Lost Steps* attempted a journey back to the primary sources of a riven cultural identity and failed. One could argue that he failed because he held a partial, and thus false, understanding of the reality of either of the Americas that he spanned. The impossibility of reconciling the fragmented elements of a self forged in the dual experience of both Americas, Latin America and the United States, is perhaps indicative of the time of the novel's publication. By the mid-1950s, the Cold War was approaching its zenith. Labor migration, which would offer a counterbalance to the overblown ideology of difference, had not yet reached its peak, and the Latin American literary boom of the 1960s that would make Gabriel García Márquez a name as well or better known within the United States than William Faulkner had not yet occurred.

Estrangement and separation were the watchwords of the 1950s, with artificial divisions strictly imposed from above: those of First World and Third World, black and white, male and female, "us" and "them," to cite the most obvious codes. From a fin de siècle perspective, North-South relations are undergoing a revisitation from a dynamic, dialectical position that demystifies old notions of the "other" that were the underpinnings of an us/them equation. This time around, demographic reality cannot be ignored. There is open acknowledgment of the Latin Americanization of the United States, its growing demographic and cultural influence, as well as an acknowledgment of internal "others" within Latin America. Literature mediates between different worlds. In and across the Americas, the terms of that mediation are constantly changing. In the late 1990s, Latin American and Latino literary production is breaking new ground. Along with the fictional imagination that has historically served as a source of resistance to domination, from the birth of the Latin American novel on, something new is taking shape. The narratives themselves are beginning to cross borders, signaling the possibility of Pan-American rapprochement.

Just as the Cuban-American narratives examined here have undertaken, in recent years, a journey of return, other hyphenated writers, from Dominican-American Julia Alvarez to Guatemalan-born Victor Perera, are crossing and recrossing borders in their works, mapping the route back. Their narratives invariably reveal the increasing influence of the diaspora on the home country. Perera's chapter titled "The New Indian versus the New Maya" analyzes the ongoing interaction between highland and lowland Mayas that is bringing to the fore complex questions of Maya identity, as well as the effects a returning diaspora will have on policy debates surrounding biculturalism and bilingual education. Along with the New Indians, those who have "exchanged a part of their identity for a place in the ladino political landscape,"[2] Perera's *Unfinished Conquest* documents the perseverance and potential impact of a Maya elite, often foreign educated, that refuses to compromise. In these and other contemporary works, the rapprochement and reconciliation achieved through the literary imagination prefigures a trend not yet officially recognized in geopolitical reality. This is nothing new in the Americas, where a syncretic literary imagination has often captured what chroniclers and analysts have failed to grasp and record.

In *The Dialectics of Our America,* Saldívar examines how Chicano border narratives "challenge the authority and even the future identity of monocultural America."[3] And in Julia Alvarez's historical novel *In the Time of the Butterflies,* which chronicles the popular resistance to the Trujillo regime, the Dominican-American interviewer's presence seems to inform the entire text, signaling emigration as an ever present, underlying subtext. It is not just because the author—who scrutinizes the nation-state and its trajectory—is herself an émigré but because she writes for both homeland and diaspora. The novel tells a story that official history could not as long as the *trujillista* legacy persisted. *In the Time of the Butterflies,* then, is a point of departure, a beginning, for the many tales that have yet to be told. Alvarez acknowledges this directly in the postscript to the novel: "To Dominicans separated by language from the world I have created, I hope this book deepens North Americans' understanding of the nightmare you endured and the heavy losses you suffered—of which this story tells only a few."[4]

It should be noted that *In the Time of the Butterflies* has, since its initial publication, been translated into Spanish and extremely well received in the Dominican Republic. In the same postscript, Alvarez notes that a "novel is not, after all, a historical document, but a way to travel through the human heart"; but it is reasonable to assume that many young Dominicans, too young to have lived through the Trujillo years or witnessed the rise of the opposition movement, are reading her narrative as both the history and pulse of a nation. The text thus immerses readers on either side of the geographic and linguistic divide in a tangled, complex, and dangerous moment in Antillean history that "can finally be understood by fiction, only finally be redeemed by the imagination" (*Butterflies,* 324).

Mexican writer Paco Ignacio Taibo's *Four Hands,* another significant novel to which we will return in greater detail, posits the novel as a vehicle for literary, cultural, and social border crossing. The "four hands" of the title are those of two journalists, one Mexican, the other from the United States, who form a team translating each other's writing into Spanish or English depending on the place of publication. The essence of their collaboration and camaraderie involves the translating of historical, social, and cultural understanding and sensibilities for the fictional audiences contained within the novel as well as the broader audience reading the novel, either in the original Spanish edition or the English translation. In its opening pages, Stan Laurel travels to Parral, where in 1923, from the window of his hotel room, he witnesses the assassination of Pancho Villa. Laurel is presented to the reader as a sympathetic gringo, someone whose demeanor "made you want to invite him to recite poetry in a duet with you." That is how he is perceived by the Mexican customs official who sees in Laurel someone "just like himself," feels "a vast bursting solidarity growing inside him," and makes "the signal to let the traveler pass freely."[5] The opening scene functions on multiple literary and symbolic levels, signaling the inherent human potential for Pan-American rapprochement and understanding that will be thwarted by officialdom, sinister and otherwise, in the twists and turns that move the novel's plot. Julio and Greg, the journalistic duo, each chronicle, catalog, and enumerate the stereotypes of their respective American nations; then, having done so, they break the stereotypes wide open with their own atypical attitudes and values. Julio is thus Mexican and Pan-American; Greg, American and Pan-American. Together, they chart and embody the promise of a distinct American future in harmony with the vision of José Martí. In his *Culture and Imperialism,* Edward Said notes in characters like Taibo's a healthy rupture with a literary past in which the novel was identified with empire: "Once we accept the actual configuration of literary experiences overlapping with one another and interdependent, despite national boundaries and coercively legislated national autonomies, history and geography are transfigured in new maps, in new and far less stable entities, in new types of connections. Exile, far from being the fate of nearly forgotten unfortunates who are dispossessed and expatriated, becomes something closer to a norm, an experience of crossing boundaries and charting new territories in defiance of the classic canonic enclosures. . . . Newly changed models and types jostle against older ones."[6]

The relationship of contemporary Latino narratives to the established corpus of twentieth-century Latin American literature and, within those categories, of Cuban-American literature to the Cuban canon, is precisely that which Said's reflections shed needed light on. The "jostling" is fruitful for both camps. In the case of Achy Obejas and Julia Alvarez, among others, the "newly changed models" both subsume and transcend the tradition from which they spring, and the young off-island writers bring to shared history, culture, and tradition a new perspective, a new language, and an illuminating critical distance. Said has further remarked that one of the functions of the public intellectual—a category that must include writers, as well—is that of alternate memory, particularly in epochs of collective "forgetting," because if knowledge of the past is silenced, then understanding of the present will be blocked. The consequences for the keepers of alternate memory, Said continues, are a kind of "exile, outsideness, marginality."[7] It is the condition of "outsideness" that permits a greater vision, from the vantage point of distance and separation, and keener insight. Barbadian-American novelist Paule Marshall defines the two central themes of her work squarely within the framework being examined here: "the importance of truly confronting the past, both in personal and historical terms, and the necessity of reversing the present order."[8] Acknowledging the wide angle of vision of the inhabitant of two, or more, worlds, Kamau Brathwaite states: "Had Paule Marshall been a West Indian, she probably would not have written [The Chosen People]. Had she not been a Afro-American of West Indian parentage, she probably could not have written it either"(quoted in Gikandi, 169).

This is the key to situating Latino and Cuban-American narratives as well, those that stand poised between origins and diaspora, scrutinizing and questioning both with equal passion and rigor. To echo Brathwaite's observations, since the same condition of *betweenness* holds, only Julia Alvarez could have written *In the Time of the Butterflies*. And only Achy Obejas, compassionately estranged from both Cuba and the Cuban exiles' enclave that her work explores, could have written *Memory Mambo*. Cuban-Americans writing in English do not, then, constitute a singular phenomenon but fall within a more far-reaching context of inter-American cultural exchange and Pan-American historical consciousness of which all the writers mentioned in this chapter form part. Their writing and the themes, old and new, it explores, feeds into a generalized movement to "expand the horizons against which questions of *how* and *what* to read and write are both posed and answered," called for by Said. Such writers are evidence, with their lucid and fertile betweenness, that the "reader and writer of literature no longer need be tied to an image of the poet or scholar in isolation, secure, stable, national in identity, class, gender or profession" (Said 1994, 317). The conscious assumption and articulation of betweenness takes many forms in literature and the arts. It has been the central theme of Mexican performance artist Guillermo Gómez Peña's monologues, performance poems, and critical essays, which take account of the Latin America that "lives and breathes in the United States and vice versa," chronicling cross-cultural fusion within the Americas at the grassroots level and forever banishing the myth of cultural purity. He calls for a new kind of cultural theory "capable of articulating our incredible circumstances" (quoted in Saldívar, 150). And also part of these circumstances are the scores of Cuban artists and intellectuals who have been defining and redefining themselves and their oeuvre on the margins since 1989, when so many accepted fellowships in Mexico, the United States, or Europe without, as prerequisite for departure, renouncing their Cubanness. Within the United States, John Sayles published *Los Gusanos* in 1991, a novel that spans six decades of one family's history in Cuba and the United States, and in which large chunks of dialogue and narrative are written entirely in Spanish, without translation. In a continued artistic effort to call attention to the need to bridge the gap that has divided the two Americas, Sayles later made a film, in Spanish, with Latin American actors, for a domestic audience.

Chicano novelist Rolando Hinojosa's Klail City Death Trip series is part of the same process of questioning the border and its meaning, examined from both sides of the divide, disputing the insular, nationalistic claim of the Texas Rangers and white settlers that the border had been "won" (see Saldívar, 49–84). Hinojosa's novels form a sweeping chronicle of Texas that explores and documents the border by continually crossing it. The two detectives of *Partners in Crime,* Rafe Buenrostro and Jehú Malacara, function as existential commuters, interpreters and mediators of two cultures, whether in Klail City; Barrones, Tamaulipas, Mexico, or Jonesville-on-the-River. The novels, reflecting the evolving circumstances of the main characters' lives, move from Spanish to English, as the two men come of age and take root. Hinojosa explains that "in the first two or three works I focus mainly on the Texas Mexican. But as both Rafe Buenrostro and Jehú Malacara grow up and go into the Army, the University of Texas and the workplace, they're coming into the Texas Anglo world" (quoted in Saldívar, 80).

Hinojosa's second novel, *Klail City y sus alrededores* (1976), was awarded the Casa de las Américas prize for the novel and published in Havana in Spanish. When an East German publisher picked up and translated the work, the translator recalls that they couldn't decide "whether to market the work as part of the Latin American program or part of the United States Literature program" (Broyles, quoted in Saldívar, 63).

A good and valid question indeed, and one that could only be formulated a continent away, in Europe. Within the United States, and despite at least a decade of multiculturalism, the boundaries that have separated and contained Latin American literature, Latino literature, African-American literature, and American literature within their own spheres still remain in evidence, at least within the academy. There is little doubt, at the close of the twentieth century, that global social reality belies such neat academic categories and will eventually render them irrelevant. Would it not be more stimulating and more reflective of American reality to mix them all up? To read Toni Morrison, Alejo Carpentier, William Faulkner, Julia Alvarez, Herman Melville, Gabriel García Márquez, and Achy Obejas, for example, recognizing that each expresses a dimension of American reality, without neglecting the specificity of race, class, and gender that differentiate experience on either side of the border? By limiting the terms of the debate to one America alone, we impoverish it, observes Michael Hanchard: "As it happens, the issues that divide and preoccupy contemporary U.S. African-American intellectuals have precursors less in the writings of Lionel Trilling, Irving Howe and Irving Kristol than in the writings and politics of Latin America and the Caribbean. People like C. L. R. James or Rigoberta Menchú of Guatemala are more apt references."[9]

Julia Alvarez holds and writes from a similar worldview, according to which "our world is becoming a place of shifting borders, where nations form and reform."[10] In the same interview, she responds as follows to the question of her own identity: "I'm not a Dominican writer. I can't pretend to be a Dominican. But by the same token, when people ask me if I'm an American writer, I have to say I don't think of myself as being in the same tradition as Melville or Hawthorne. I'm a hyphenated person interested in the music that comes out of a language that hears with both languages. My stories come out of being in worlds that sometimes clash and sometimes combine." And Jorge Semprun, in his most recent book, *Literature or Life,* a cross between memoir and literary essay, frames the question in terms that go straight to the heart of this exploration of Cuban writers on and off the island: "French was just as much my mother tongue, in fact, as Spanish. It had become so, at least. I hadn't chosen the place where I was born, the native soil of my native language. Nationality: this thing, or idea, or reality for which so many have fought, spilling so much blood, is the thing that least belongs to you, the most accidental."[11]

It is in the spirit of Semprun's reflections that this volume has been conceived in terms of Cuban writers forming a continuum, whether on or off the island, rather than following the more definitive and divisive categorization of *Cuban* and *Cuban-American* literature. Emphasizing Cubanness, in the sense of a cultural tradition shared by canonic and diaspora writers alike, as the common denominator in the corpus of works studied makes possible a shift in focus toward dialogue rather than opposition. All the writers examined sense, at work within themselves, a dialectic of cultures that in turn serves as the motivating force for the literary imagination. Although the narrative resolutions of a hyphenated imagination differ in each of the literary works, the impetus that moves them toward, and inserts them within, a growing Pan-American consciousness is the same. Carpentier makes his dual Cuban and European formation a central theme of all his later, mature novels from *Los pasos perdidos* to his last two works, *Consagración de la primavera* and *El harpa y la sombra,* novels in which the protagonists move along a here/there axis to reveal two cultural worlds in juxtaposition, whether Latin America and Europe or Latin America and the United States. Julia Alvarez marks and explores the historical roots of a dual heritage in the thematic trajectory of her novels themselves. In *How the García Girls Lost Their Accents,* the characters move back and forth from the present of a

New York girlhood to their Dominican childhood—their origins before displacement. Her second novel, *In the Time of the Butterflies,* explores the historical context of that emigration, the profound spiritual and social consequences for each individual who endured the collective experience of the Trujillo regime and its opposition. Her third novel, *¡Yo!,* returns to the United States to focus on the lives of Dominican émigrés, now adults, and examine the complex relationship of an émigré writer to U.S. culture and the culture of her native island, as well as the relationship of literature to history and literature to life itself: the creative process that transforms the raw material of lived experience into art.

The messy, problematic nature of the relationship of history to literature in the Americas is the glue that holds the myriad of fragments, narratives, characters, and parallel or intersecting plots together in Taibo's border-crossing *Four Hands.* Like Alvarez herself, Taibo's characters articulate their frustration with the insufficiency of any single genre or medium to capture and articulate American reality, a recurring professional journalist's crisis for protagonists Julio ("Fats") and Greg: "Fats appeared with a bottle of Spanish cognac taken from his marvelous bag and proposed that we screw journalism once and for all and dedicate ourselves to writing a novel, or to living. This was a crisis that occurred regularly. . . . A crisis that was based on the horrors of a profession in which one tells the stories that others, normal people, people with passions are living" (*Four Hands,* 39).

Julio and Greg tell fragments of their story—revealed in the conclusion to be the novel "they would never write"—against a disjointed collage of narratives that ramble across continents and decades, assembling, as they unwind, a collection of characters who insert themselves into the great political dramas of the twentieth century. Stan Laurel and Pancho Villa, the veterans of the International Brigades of the Spanish civil war, Mexican drug traffickers, Nicaraguan revolutionaries and CIA henchmen—as the novel progresses, their lives come together, entangled within an ambitious CIA plot that involves a rewriting of the past to alter present and future events. Another character, Elena Jordan, punctuates the narrative collage with her rejected thesis proposals, all dealing with the potential connections to be made across the unofficial geography and unwritten history of Latin America, better suited to the baroque imagination at work in Carpentier's theory of the marvelous-real than to the formal requirements of a doctoral dissertation. The other device that points to the insufficiency of any one genre or discipline is the novel within the novel, Emilio Salgari's version of *Goodbye to*

Mompracem, a Malaysian-Portuguese adventure of swashbuckling resistance to European imperial ambitions. The last episode in the parallel novel reaffirms the protagonists' conviction that history never ends, that words never fall into a void, that the good fight will always be continued by a generation to come. In the same spirit, on a visit to the Aztec ruins at Teotihuacán, Julio and Greg envision the construction of a new, Pan-American country, emerging from the combined ruins of the old. It is a vision sharper and more prescient than the hybrid no-man's-land concentrated on the border conjured by Carlos Fuentes in *Cristóbal Nonato*:

> "It's the Mexicans' turn for a return to glory. If we're going to make a country, it's got to be by mixing the ruins of this with the ruins of Mexico City."
> "I'll lend you Hollywood Boulevard to add to it and you'll make a beautiful country."
> Julio kept thinking about it, the idea didn't entirely bother him. We had traveled through too much countryside, crossed too many borders to take customs and borders, barbed-wire fences and passports seriously. (*Four Hands,* 278)

In counterpoint to the CIA plots that distort and divide the Americas, *Four Hands* charts an alternate terrain of Pan-American comprehension and collaboration. Love crosses all linguistic and national frontiers, taking many forms, binding together the text's many unlikely pairs of inter-American friends, colleagues, and lovers.

Toward the novel's conclusion, several key episodes set within the United States offer a portrait of the illegal aliens from across the border, the "invisibles," who make this country run. Taibo's novel gives them a biography, projects them into history, renders them *visible* and *defiant* of an assimilationist mandate for total integration, a condition that can be met only by self-denial or, alternately, descent into the depths of Dantean circles of hell:

> They were looking for the same thing they could offer: a tribe, a clan to protect them from inclement weather, attacks, illegal labor, loneliness and unemployment. It could have been those three Puerto Rican saleswomen at Mart's, an electronics store in the middle of the block, if it weren't that the Puerto Rican electronic girls were in social ascent in a society that measures its waves of new citizens by their proximity to the unreal center of a circle of integration. . . . At that point, the electronic girls were on the eighth interior circle and the invisibles on the twelfth at best. Nothing there. (*Four Hands,* 313)

Illegality, displacement, and the misguided official inter-American relations in which these conditions originate structure Demetria Martínez's first novel, *MotherTongue*. In it, a young Mexican-American woman and a clandestine Salvadoran, a political refugee from his nation's civil war, build bridges that span the Americas from their lives, their voices, their individual and collective histories. Central to the work are the redemptive power of language and literature, and the hidden but ever present history of a Pan-American unity that defies the authority of borders and visas: "Here is a poem José Luis wrote, dated August 13, 1982. As part of a Spanish lesson, he had me translate it. We kept several dictionaries on the kitchen table. Dodging from word to word for hours at a sitting, we made our way across borders of language without passports or permits. . . . romantic dreams, yes, but the kind that dwell side by side with resistance. The space we cleared on the kitchen table to do translations, near folders and clippings about El Salvador, was a magic circle. It was beyond law and order."[12]

In the works of Latin American and Latino authors Taibo, Alvarez, and Martínez, as in the corpus of Cuban-American narratives addressed in the previous chapter, émigrés are *displaced* but do *not* burn their bridges upon arrival in a new land. The twentieth-century remaking of immigrant lives within the Americas occurs within an unbroken flow that connects origins and diaspora, moving back and forth across two cultures, two sets of history and tradition. These are tales of syncretism rather than renunciation. Esmeralda Santiago's *When I Was Puerto Rican* (1993) stands as an exception. As the title suggests, her testimonial is reminiscent of earlier immigrant narratives in which the characters become American by ceasing to be *other* in a process of acculturation based on self-denial, rather than the fluid, syncretic transculturation chronicled in the works selected for this study—works in which bilingualism and biculturalism serve as the basis for an ongoing literary dialogue that integrates the past and the present and points toward a Pan-American future. At worst, contemporary Latino narratives posit exile or displacement as a variant on György Lukács's formulation in *The Theory of the Novel* of the novel as existential homelessness. If, as Said argues in *Culture and Imperialism,* the novel has been literature's most favored site for expressing nationalism and imperial consciousness, then for the displaced writer, caught between two worlds, literature may express, rather, a condition of being ill at ease in the world.

That is certainly the case for the characters that populate Paris-based Zoë Valdés's debut novel *La nada cotidiana* (1995). It is an existentialist novel of a nihilistic bent, and the significance of the title, with its emphasis on *nothingness,* the *void,* the *emptiness* of the everyday, both echoes and goes beyond that evoked by Parisian novelist Boris Vian's *L'écume des jours* (1963). The text opens with a parable that frames the first-person narrative that follows, and the phrase, in the third person, "She comes from an island that wanted to construct paradise."[13] The novel closes with the protagonist's macabre, prophetic vision of "thousands of cadavers on rafts, floating in the ocean" (*La nada,* 171; translation mine), followed by a circular repetition of the opening phrase.

Between the first and last evocations of a paradise manqué unfolds a first-person existentialist novel that spans, chronologically, exactly the course of the Cuban revolution, from 1959 (the year of the narrator's, and the novelist's, birth) to the present. Trapped in the emptiness of the quotidian, in a void made up of identical days, and caught between two lovers, the Traitor and the Nihilist, Patria, whose name means "homeland," seeks a way out through writing. Like the first-person narrator of Desnoes's existential novel written 30 years earlier, *Memorias del subdesarrollo,* Valdés's protagonist Patria writes *against* an alienating social landscape in which nationalism and *patria* have for her lost all meaning. Unlike Desnoes's 1965 novel, however, in Valdés's 1995 novel it is not the shock of radical change that transforms an erstwhile complacency into numb alienation. Valdés has structured an existential novel not on the axis of the generation that made the revolution but on that of their children: the promise of the future, of continuity. Patria, born with the revolution, comes of age with it, suffers disillusionment and fragmentation, and comes to an impasse along with a revolutionary process that parallels the course of her life. Desnoes's narrator ultimately finds no solace in his journal keeping and, weary of writing, declares his desire "to go beyond words," to surmount his existential crisis by propelling himself into a life of action, of social engagement. For Valdés's disillusioned 1990s protagonist, the ideal of a life of action wedded to shared social and moral values is no longer an option. On the island, freedom and liberation are attainable, not through an activism rendered, over time, devoid of meaning, but rather in words, "words that, like madwomen, whores, fairies, goddesses, explode wildly along with the ink from the pen that my fingers grip" (*La nada,* 171; translation mine).

All is contained, memorialized, within the suprahistorical realm of the word: "Because great friends have died, others have left, and others remain. All are here within me. Within the words I no longer know if I write. Or if they write me" (*La nada,* 171; translation mine). Thus, in the conclusion to her novel, Valdés alludes powerfully to *emigration* and *absence*—among the strongest emerging themes in contemporary Cuban fiction being produced on the island as well.

Miguel Barnet's short story "Miosvatis," the central fiction piece in *The New Yorker*'s January 1998 "Cuba Issue," deals with absence on another level and from a distinct perspective. Returning to the classic theme of the "home" and the "world," and the tension between the two that recurs in twentieth-century literature, the protagonist, like many Cuban artists and writers, exists in a state of flux between the two, continually ill at ease. The narrative posits Cuba as *absence* in the protagonist's consciousness, whether he is in Zurich or Havana, on the labyrinthine errand that causes him to take stock of the city, *his* city. Cuba is alternately *absence,* when at home, or *nostalgia* that fills the spirit and imagination of the narrator as he moves about under the gray skies of Zurich, and later through the streets of Paris, the "gray elephant," until he finally boards an Iberia airliner back to Havana. Once home, bearing gifts for his German friend's Cuban lover—another compelling absence that informs the narrative, since he never actually catches up with her—he discovers that the telephone in his apartment has been out of service since he left for Europe: "I resigned myself. 'Fine,' I said. 'Now my stay in Europe will be extended, since without a telephone I'm simply not here, I am no one, one who has not yet arrived.' "[14]

Havana is a landscape of estrangement: a place where the dogs don't bark, the clock has stopped, every encounter becomes a disjuncture, and the interiors of the apartments he walks into on his quest appear to the narrator to be stage sets. Everything, and everyone, seems to be in a state of suspended animation, waiting for the action to resume, for the spark of change that will connect what was with what will be. As the protagonist winds his way through narrow streets to the *barrio* Colón, the neighborhood where the recipient of the gifts lives, his multiple encounters with strangers produce inquiries about his nationality. To the persistent questions, he responds calmly that he is not German, not Spanish, that he is Cuban:

> "No, Ma'am, I'm Cuban . . ."
> "Ah, Cuban! But you live outside."
> "No, Ma'am, I live here, and I've come to bring a present for your neighbor." ("Miosvatis," 71)

In this, the most recent short story by Barnet, one of Cuba's most celebrated contemporary writers, Cuba is a site of estrangement, and the narrator's condition is one of seemingly permanent in-betweenness, despite his protestations to the contrary; he is nostalgic for Havana when in Europe, yet hauntingly estranged from the city upon his return and reinsertion into the life of the island. The story ends with a streetscape, like a snapshot, an image of the timeworn yet still magnificent Malecón, the seawall usually bustling with Cubans sitting, strolling, fishing, talking; Cubans now oddly absent under Havana's noonday sun: "At that hour, the Malecón was almost deserted. Only a tourist couple in Bermuda shorts and a sad and sickly dog, like Giacometti's, were silhouetted against the landscape" ("Miosvatis," 74).

Such literature clearly shatters the ease and familiarity of the "home," the nation, now viewed from the critical distance of betweenness. Unburdened by nostalgia, a new wave of Cuban-American narrators are also now free to engage actively, and critically, with the reality that surrounds them, giving full rein to, rather than denying, the contradictions inherent in a hyphenated life and vision, as their counterparts on the island, whether consecrated or emerging writers, take stock of the moment, the current impasse, that instant, captured as if in slow motion, before things shift and resume their course.

Conclusion

A decade ago, this study could not have been written, primarily because my interest in the literature of the diaspora, the "off-island" Cubans, had not yet been awakened. As a doctoral student, I immersed myself in the study of the Cuban canon, exclusively, conducting research on the island. I had grown allergic, in the academic climate of the United States, to the polarization of Cuban literary expression, and corresponding literary studies, into two ideological camps: the literature of the revolution and the literature of the exile. The lines of separation had been drawn in such a way that Cuban literature, produced both on the island and by the diaspora, was forced into two parallel, conceptual universes. Back then, had a study that brought the many strains of Cuban literature together in a universalist spirit been written, it might not have found an audience. The Cold War fostered sectarianism, but much water has passed under the bridge since its official demise. World maps have been drawn and redrawn since 1989 to account for shifting borders. And shifting borders bring about shifts in concepts and consciousness, a rethinking of the established across disciplines. It is only logical that approaches to Cuban literature, wherever it is produced, also undergo direct and subtle adaptations in keeping with the contours of a changing world. Acknowledgment of, or perhaps a return to, the useful virtues of interdisciplinarity and cultural hybridity is creating new grounds for literature and literary studies. Canonical enclosure is giving way to elasticity and innovation. In the case of Cuba, whereas panels on Cuban politics, society, and arts and letters invariably used to degenerate into shouting matches, with one camp attempting to impose its monologue on the other, the miracle of dialogue is slowly but inexorably beginning to occur. An examination of contemporary Cuban writing, structured as a literary conversation between canon and diaspora, is one more effort to contribute to and shape the dialogue now taking place. Books dialogue with other books, it is said, and each generation dialogues with the one that came before it.

This study builds, in the same way, on those that came before it, documenting continuity and growth in my own scholarship, which has been enriched by the works of others. I first took on Cuban literary history as a continuum in my 1987 study. Unwilling to segment that history into a *before* and an *after* the revolution, I studied literary expression as it evolved over the course of a century. My next major project, an anthology of contemporary literature of the Caribbean, sought to break down the colonialist barriers that have been drawn around the English-, Spanish-, and French-language literatures of the region, tying them in static and unilateral fashion to their respective metropolises. I have thus gained experience, as a scholar, in establishing common ground, rebuilding bridges or devising alternate ones, and seeking out conceptual links as the basis for literary study. History provides the key; if one takes the long historical view of a region's, nation's, or community's literary expression, the connections reveal themselves. Guillermo Cabrera Infante, one of Cuba's major contemporary novelists, reveals in *Mea Cuba* how essential is the dynamic of history: "A country is not just geography. It is also history." When he returned from Brussels, where he served as cultural attaché, to Havana in 1965, he encountered a void where history had been: "In Cuba, the moon was shining as before the Revolution, the sun was the same sun: nature lent everything its eponymous beauty. Geography was alive, but history had died."[1]

Admittedly, for Cabrera Infante, the perception that history had died on the island meant that all his bridges to it had been "burned." For other literary figures before and after, the bridges remain—however tenuously—allowing for and inviting a journey of return. Ultimately, this study came to be based on their narratives. Over the course of the extensive period of reading and research that went into the preparation for this book, I discovered that, thematically, the writers who had not burned their bridges intrigued me most. This study, then, is built around their work and the structural and historical theme of rapprochement. Islands invite leaps and hurtles, to elsewhere and back, or not. On terra firma, borders shift, move, are redrawn; on islands, the borders remain fixed, barring erosion of the landmass or natural disaster; it is the population that is fluid. For every islander who leaves, there is one who remains, and vice versa. Renée Méndez Capote, author of *Memorias de una cubanita que nació con el siglo,* a marvelous chronicle of the first decades in the life of the Cuban republic, remained on the island. Yet given the mobility of her class, she might just as well not have, and her narrative would have captured the experiences, the "memories of a Cuban girl who was born with the century and left," as so many Cubans did in the decades of the 1930s and 1940s. Those are the narratives contained within Barnet's testimonial novel of Cuban life in New York, *La vida real,* and Brooklyn-based artist Julio Girona's testimonial account of his experiences as a volunteer in the U.S. Army during World War II, *Seis horas y más*. Even Cabrera Infante selected as the epigraph for *Mea Cuba* Martí's tribute to the unity of culture and tradition that transcends displacement, "Cuba unites us all on foreign soil."

My first chapter, "The Home and the World," traces an uninterrupted history of displacement among island-born Cubans, taking Alejo Carpentier and Achy Obejas as markers on a transnational literary map, one that encompasses, from the onset and on principle, the island and the émigrés, the canon and the diaspora. Cuba's literature has, from its earliest beginnings, chronicled displacement and return, from Villaverde's classic *Cecilia Valdés,* completed toward the end of the last century and published on foreign soil, to Carpentier's and Barnet's novelistic leaps off the island and back, across historical epochs. From 1492 onward, the Caribbean has been "imperial frontier," a site of conflict and crossroads of the universe. The task of situating contemporary Cuban literature requires that we take the same conceptual leaps its creators have, from the island to the ends of the world and back.

Having placed the twentieth-century literary tradition in context, chapter 2, "Building the Cuban Canon," examines the emergence and development of major themes in contemporary Cuban literature in the novels of selected major and transitional figures: Alejo Carpentier, José Lezama Lima, Miguel Barnet, Renée Méndez Capote, Pablo Armando Fernández, Edmundo Desnoes and Reinaldo Arenas. Arenas, who began his trajectory as a novelist in Cuba and continued it in New York after he emigrated, serves as bridge to chapter 3, "Canon and Diaspora: A Literary Dialogue."

In looking at the literary production of writers of the canon and the diaspora, the impact of *la novela-testimonio* on historiography and fictional narrative is significant. Testimonial novel or narrative, the genre that enjoyed a strong resurgence in the 1960s, reemerged in that decade as counterpoint to its colonial roots in the chronicles of the conquerors. It is no accident that many of the genre's practitioners were Cuban, or that the genre gained momentum in the 1960s, in a climate that favored revision, revisitation, and critical rethinking of the bases for literary creation, historiography, identity and representation, cultural practices, and the arts, in general. Individual and collective memory; history and consciousness: these are the thematic and structural motifs of the testimonial and historical novels of Cuba's leading literary figures. They also emerge as the literary themes of the contemporary diaspora writers studied here, either as central or tangential threads in the works of Achy Obejas, Oscar Hijuelos, Cristina García, Virgil Suárez, Roberto G. Fernández, and Marisella Veiga. As a corpus, their narratives explore generational difference, contradiction, disjuncture, identity, and self-representation. They pose the existential question of what it means to be Cuban in a land and a language distinct from that of parents and origins; their characters register degrees of integration into, or alienation from, the culture of the enclave. In the writings of a contemporary off-island generation, in the 1990s, questions of race, class, and gender in the context of the United States bump up against their meanings in the "old" world of the island and its historical trajectory, producing critical clarity for some and alienation for others. Their works, in the development of an original cast of Cuban and American characters, and the universe within which they move and interact, often attain a brilliant, existential clarity.

The fourth and final chapter, "From Lost Steps to Hyphenated Lives," examines contemporary Cuban voices within the larger context of Latino literature and the stretching of the American canon, of which they form part. "Hyphenated," or "transplanted" writers, Latin American émigrés and their children, living and working (more often than not in English) outside of Latin America and the Caribbean, are now exerting an influence on both adopted and home countries. The emphasis is on "transplanted" or second-, third-, and even fourth-generation Latin Americans within the United States as heirs to, and "continuers" of, a literary tradition. With roots in the rich literary culture of Latin America, they transform and enrich the tradition of the region with their hyphenated voices, their bilingual, bicultural sensibilities and experience. Along with hyphenated writers such as Dominican-American Julia Alvarez and Mexican-Americans Rolando Hinojosa and Demetria Martínez, I include the United States' John Sayles and Mexico's Paco Ignacio Taibo and Guillermo Gómez Peña, who have embarked on a journey of border crossing to uncover a fin de siècle American aesthetic and reveal in the process what unites as well as divides the two Americas.

Noted, as well, is the emerging tendency of U.S. artists and academics to acknowledge and address the Latin Americanization of the United States, the "other" America to José Martí's "Our America," and to look to Latin America and the Caribbean's cultural theorists as well as their own for conceptual tools and sources of meaning. Throughout, the problematic relationship of the literary and the historical imaginations is manifest, on either side of the border, as well as the redemptive power of language and the arts. Engagement begins to replace nostalgia and evocation for a powerful new generation of Latino narrators. Cuban cultural theorist Roberto Fernández Retamar's *Caliban and Other Essays* and Chicano theorist José David Saldívar's *The Dialectics of Our America: Genealogy, Cultural Critique, and Literary History* serve as the conceptual framework for the concluding chapter. Controversial and original, each broke new ground and set the terms of debate for a generation; Retamar in the early 1970s, and Saldívar for the 1990s. Both sought to redefine American consciousness and the limits of inter-American comprehension and exchange. Saldívar assesses the legacy of revisionist scholarship that has "shattered the traditional consensus." Unlike the conservative opponents of a new cultural history who believe that revisionist scholarship has gone too far afield, Saldívar argues that there has not been enough of it. For him, the fracturing or shattering of established consensus is a phase in the process of making the literary history of the Americas "whole again." Thus, for Saldívar, fragmentation is not an end in itself but the means to envisioning wholeness in new terms; a clearing of the air, and a clearing away of artificial bases of unity in search of more substantive common ground: "By looking at the Americas as a hemisphere and by analyzing the real and rhetorical, often hostile, battles between the United States and what Martí called "Nuestra América"—"Our America"—it is possible to perceive what the literatures of the Americas have in common."[2]

Employing a methodology imbued with the spirit of Saldívar's critical and theoretical quest for new and rigorous bases for commonality, this study has attempted to go beyond the "real" and "rhetorical" battles waged in the terrain of culture that have served to deepen the artificial divide separating Cubans on the island from those of the diaspora. In truth, the dominant literary themes in the works of young writers in Cuba and their counterparts in the diaspora have begun increasingly to overlap. Emigration, division, and fragmentation, once extremely rare topics in Cuban literature produced on the island, are gaining ascendancy as the economic and social crisis prolongs itself, with no immediate end in sight. Gay themes, anathema to the *machista* and paternalistic core of Cuban culture on either side of the divide, are also making significant inroads in late-twentieth-century literary production, as evidenced by the forthcoming collection of gay short stories by Pedro de Jesús, among others. The artistic and literary production of island and diaspora has for too long been perceived as developing within two separate and parallel chronologies; this study is an attempt to illuminate the cultural, critical, and intellectual spaces or points where they have and will continue to intersect.

After acknowledging where contemporary Cuban literature and the literature of the diaspora diverge, their points of fracture and tension, perhaps Cuban literary history may now begin to be made whole again, as Saldívar proposes, within the larger context of the literary history of the Americas. Recognition of plurality does not preclude the need for establishing common ground. Saldívar's vision stresses the need to establish commonality through a process of critical thought rather than superficial rhetoric. In the afterword to Amaryll Chanady's edited volume *Latin American Identity and Constructions of Difference,* Alberto Moreira joins Saldívar in lamenting that we are still too conceptually confined by European notions, not yet hybrid enough, for the enormous critical challenges of the future: "What is identity for the Quechua language? How does a speaker of Yucatec Maya relate to identity thinking? In the endless circulation of signs and concepts that organizes the possibility of cultural production today we are still not hybrid enough, not multicultural enough. Our hegemony, the one that lives through us, is the one that dictates hybridity and multiculturalism, any and all thoughts of counterhegemonic plurality as a means to keep the night of the world in place. The task of critical thinking has barely started."[3]

For Cuban literary and cultural history, the task of critical rethinking—the dialectical reworking of the seminal writings of Martí and Fernández Retamar—has begun and will no doubt gain strength and clarity in coming years. In *The Dialectics of Our America,* Saldívar states as one of the work's myriad goals that of continuing a "new line of comparative American studies extending from Roberto Fernández Retamar to such recent commentators as Vera Kutzinski, Lois Parkinson Zamora, and Gustavo Pérez Firmat" (Saldívar, xi). Cuban-American Pérez Firmat has contributed in his own right to the debate on Cuba, culture, and Cuban culture within the evolving relationship of the two Americas in *Life on the Hyphen: The Cuban-American Way.*

Mention should be made as well of works by non-Latino authors that examine the Latin Americanization of U.S. culture. David Rieff's *The Exile: Cuba in the Heart of Miami* (1993) and Joan Didion's *Miami* (1987) cast their gaze on the enclave from without. Insiders may debate whether the authors, as outsiders, have understood or misunderstood the process of transculturation at work in the lives of hyphenated Cubans. However, attention to the topic by writers outside the enclave itself is evidence that the Cuban presence is once again a force and focus of attention in U.S., European, and Latin American cultural life at the end of this century, as it was in 1898—particularly as Cuba undertakes the process of repositioning itself globally.

The shifts now occurring are bilateral; the Cuban diaspora is also engaged in a process of rethinking its position in international terms. The range of literary settings found in the new Cuban-American narratives reflects this. Achy Obejas's novelistic universe encompasses Chicago, Mexico, New York, Havana, *and* Miami, almost as afterthought. Virgil Suárez's characters develop in diverse contexts that range from Miami to the Southwest, Miami to California, and Miami to Cuba itself in *Going Under*. In Suárez's fiction, Miami is not a destination but a dead end from which the characters must extricate themselves in order to survive. In "Fresh Fruit," Marisella Veiga situates her characters on an unnamed Antillean island, locating Cuban identity in the Caribbean, not Miami.

At a PEN-sponsored panel on the evolution of Latino writing over the last 20 years, Dolores Prida observed that Latino literature began when hyphenated or transplanted writers stopped writing about Latin America and began writing about themselves. Panelist Miguel Algarín reminded the audience that New York has always been a Caribbean, Latin American city, that even in the 1890s half of New York's theater productions were in Spanish, and the other half in English.[4] In the late 1990s, Latino cultural influence is recognized outside its historical centers of concentration within the United States, extending throughout the country, including the Cuban presence outside of Miami.

Within Cuba, the literary history of the twentieth century has been marked by cycles of rupture and continuity. Moments of upheaval, change, and uncertainty have often been accompanied by a hiatus, a cathartic silence in literary culture, followed by renewed production, as occurred in the 1920s and 1930s, following 1898 and its aftermath. Based on its cyclical development in the past, it seems likely that Cuba's literary production will experience another hiatus, a period of incubation preceding a strong resurgence of the novel that will chronicle, in diverse forms, formats, and thematic content, the final half of the present century. The works of young writers on the island, just now emerging, would seem to indicate that the resurgence has already begun, although international dissemination of their works beyond the island's parameters is still problematic.

The coming century should witness an even greater rapprochement and resonance between the Cuban literary canon and the literature of the diaspora, as fresh critical voices within both camps explore their changing reality and assume the task of reflecting the past and present of their own generational experience, with an eye toward the future. With greater numbers of Cuban émigrés traveling to the island in recent years, increasing levels of exchange make nostalgia in its purest form a relic of the literary past. *Memory Mambo,* in shattering the myths of false memory, claims uncharted territory for the novel and constitutes a kind of swan song for a Cuban-American literature of evocation that avoids confrontation with present reality. Free of the artificial coherence provided by the alienated and alienating mythology of the Cuban enclave that Roberto G. Fernández dismantles in his novelistic collage of Miami, the characters descend into total fragmentation. From the fragments of a shifting reality for Cubans on and off the island, a new language, a distinct medium of communication, is being forged; and through it, a new literary dialogue can begin.

Notes and References

Preface

　　1.　Antonio Benítez Rojo, *The Repeating Island: The Caribbean and the Postmodern Perspective,* trans. James Maraniss (Durham, N.C.: Duke University Press, 1992), 5.

　　2.　Édouard Glissant, *Caribbean Discourse: Selected Essays,* trans. J. Michael Dash (Charlottesville: University Press of Virginia, 1989), xxxix.

　　3.　Angel Rama, *La novela en América Latina: Panoramas, 1920–1980* (Bogotá: Instituto Colombiano de Cultura, 1982), 194, translation mine.

　　4.　Rubén Rumbaut, "The Post-exile Generation," *Cuban Affairs* 3 (Summer–Fall 1996): 5; hereafter cited in the text.

Chapter One

　　1.　Ramón Gutiérrez and Genaro Padilla, eds., *Recovering the U.S. Hispanic Literary Heritage* (Houston: Arte Público Press, 1993), 21–22.

　　2.　Achy Obejas, *We Came All the Way from Cuba So You Could Dress like This?* (Pittsburgh: Cleiss Press, 1994), 121; hereafter cited in the text as *We Came.*

　　3.　Alejo Carpentier, prologue to *The Kingdom of This World,* trans. Alfred MacAdam, in *Review: Latin American Literature and the Arts* 47 (Fall 1993): 31.

　　4.　Edmundo Desnoes, ed., *Los dispositivos en la flor: Cuba, Literatura desde la revolución* (Hanover: Ediciones del Norte, 1981), xvi, translation mine.

　　5.　Julia Alvarez, quoted in Eduardo Lago, "De un lado el Sultán, de otro la narradora: Conversación con Julia Alvarez," *Brújula/Compass,* February 1992, 16; translation mine.

　　6.　Julia Alvarez, "Grounds for Fiction," lecture, New York Public Library, 18 February 1997.

Chapter Two

　　1.　Raymond D. Souza, *Major Cuban Novelists: Innovation and Tradition* (Columbia: University of Missouri Press, 1976), 24; hereafter cited in the text as Souza 1976.

　　2.　Alejo Carpentier, *The Lost Steps,* trans. Harriet de Onís (New York: Noonday Press, 1989), 18; hereafter cited in the text as *Lost Steps.*

　　3.　One theory attributes Lezama Lima's semimarginalization to the fact that there was no mention of the revolution in *Paradiso,* together with the text's frank discussion of homosexuality, causing Lezama to fall out of official favor following the novel's publication. Other interpretations relate it to his involvement with the Padilla affair. As I mentioned, he has recently been rehabilitated on the island in the "stretching" of the canon occurring there.

4. José Lezama Lima, *Paradiso*, edición crítica, ed. Cintio Vitier (Buenos Aires: Colección Archivos, 1988), xix. Lezama Lima is quoted in "Introducción," translation mine.

5. Pedro Simón, ed., *Recopilación de textos sobre José Lezama Lima* (Havana: Casa de las Américas, 1970), 222, translation mine; hereafter cited in the text.

6. Dinorah Hernández Lima, *Versiones y re-versiones históricas en la obra de Cabrera Infante* (Madrid: Editorial Pliegos, 1990), 38, translation mine.

7. Ambrosio Fornet, ed., *Antología del cuento cubano contemporáneo* (Mexico: Ediciones Era, 1967), 35, translation mine.

8. Miguel Barnet, "La novela-testimonio: Socioliteratura," in *La canción de Rachel* (Barcelona: Editorial Estela, 1970), 125–50, 137, translation mine.

9. Pablo Armando Fernández, *Los niños se despiden* (Buenos Aires: Centro Editor de América Latina, 1971), 8, translation mine; hereafter cited in the text as *Los niños*.

10. Renée Méndez Capote, *Memorias de una cubanita que nació con el siglo* (Havana: Bolsilibros Unión, 1964), 1, translation mine; hereafter cited in the text as *Memorias de una cubanita*.

11. Edmundo Desnoes, *Inconsolable Memories*, translated by the author (New York: New American Library, 1967), 14–15; hereafter cited in the text as *Inconsolable*.

12. Reinaldo Arenas, *El mundo alucinante* (Mexico: Editorial Diógenes, 1973), 9, translation mine; hereafter cited in the text as *El mundo*.

Chapter Three

1. Neil Larsen, *Reading North by South: On Latin American Literature, Culture, and Politics* (Minneapolis: University of Minnesota Press, 1995), 162.

2. Angel Fernández Guerra, "Cimarrón y Rachel: Un continuum," in *Nuevos críticos cubanos,* ed. José Prats Sariol (Havana: Letras Cubanas, 1983), 528–37, 529, translation mine; hereafter cited in the text.

3. Miguel Barnet, *Rachel's Song,* trans. W. Nick Hill (Willamantic, Conn.: Curbstone, 1991), 9; hereafter cited in the text.

4. Alejo Carpentier, "Carpentier sobre *El siglo de las luces*," in *El siglo de las luces,* ed. Ambrosio Fornet (Madrid: Ediciones Cátedra, 1989), 42–57, 57, translation mine; hereafter cited in the text as "Carpentier sobre *El siglo.*"

5. Irlemar Champi, cited in Ambrosio Fornet, "Introducción," in *El siglo de las luces,* 13–41, 36, translation mine.

6. Miguel Barnet, *La vida real* (Madrid: Ediciones Alfaguara, 1984), 14, translation mine.

7. William Luis, *Literary Bondage: Slavery in Cuban Narrative* (Austin: University of Texas Press, 1990), 199; hereafter cited in the text as Luis 1990.

8. Achy Obejas, *Memory Mambo* (Pittsburgh: Cleis Press, 1996), 9; hereafter cited in the text.

9. Rafael Yglesias, *Dr. Neruda's Cure for Evil* (New York: Warner Books, 1996), 33.

10. Gustavo Pérez Firmat, *Life on the Hyphen: The Cuban-American Way* (Austin: University of Texas Press, 1994), 136; hereafter cited in the text as Pérez Firmat 1994.

11. Cristina García, *Dreaming in Cuban* (New York: Ballantine Books, 1993), 137–38; hereafter cited in the text as *Dreaming*.

12. Cristina García, "Dreaming in Cuban: An Interview with Cristina García," interview by Iraida H. López, *Brújula/Compass*, no. 16 (Spring 1993): 15–17, 16.

13. Virgil Suárez, *Welcome to the Oasis and Other Stories* (Houston: Arte Público Press, 1992), 54.

14. Virgil Suárez, "Settlements," in *Iguana Dreams: New Latino Fiction*, ed. Delia Poey and Virgil Suárez (New York: HarperPerennial, 1992), 297–320, 300; hereafter cited in the text.

15. Virgil Suárez, *Going Under* (Houston: Arte Público Press, 1996), 300; hereafter cited in the text.

16. Roberto G. Fernández, *La vida es un special, .75* (Miami: Ediciones Universal, 1981), 1, translation mine; hereafter cited in the text as *La vida*. In this collage of a bilingual novel, paragraphs, sentences, and even single worlds alternate wildly between Spanish and English. I have translated those passages that appear entirely in Spanish and left bilingual passages as they appear in the original wherever I believed that their meaning would be intelligible to a non-Spanish-speaking reader.

17. Marisella Veiga, "Fresh Fruit," in *Iguana Dreams: New Latino Fiction*, ed. Delia Poey and Virgil Suárez (New York: HarperPerennial, 1992), 351–53, 351; hereafter cited in the text.

Chapter Four

1. Roberto Fernández Retamar, *Caliban and Other Essays*, trans. Edward Baker (Minneapolis: University of Minnesota Press, 1989), 53.

2. Victor Perera, *Unfinished Conquest: The Guatemalan Tragedy* (Berkeley: University of California Press, 1993), 318.

3. José David Saldívar, *The Dialectics of Our America: Genealogy, Cultural Critique, and Literary History* (Durham, N.C.: Duke University Press, 1991), 84.

4. Julia Alvarez, *In the Time of the Butterflies* (New York: Plume, 1994), 324; hereafter cited in the text as *Butterflies*.

5. Paco Ignacio Taibo II, *Four Hands,* trans. Laura C. Dail (New York: St. Martin's Press, 1990), 4; hereafter cited in the text.

6. Edward Said, *Culture and Imperialism* (New York: Vintage, 1994), 317; hereafter cited in the text as Said 1994.

7. Edward Said, "Speaking Truth to Power: The Public Intellectual at the End of the Twentieth Century," roundtable discussion with Edward Said, Susan Sontag, and Juan Goytisolo, New York University, 18 April 1997.

8. Paule Marshall, quoted in Simon Gikandi, *Writing in Limbo: Modernism and Caribbean Literature* (Ithaca, N.Y.: Cornell University Press, 1992), 168; Gikandi's study hereafter cited in the text.

9. Michael Hanchard, "Intellectual Pursuit," *The Nation,* 19 February 1996, 22–24, 22.

10. Julia Alvarez, "Conversation with Julia Alvarez," interview by Heather Rosario-Sievert, *Review: Latin American Literature and the Arts* 54 (Spring 1997): 31–37, 33.

11. Jorge Semprun, *Literature or Life,* trans. Linda Coverdale (New York: Viking, 1997), 274.

12. Demetria Martínez, *MotherTongue* (Tempe, Ariz.: Bilingual Press, 1994), 43.

13. Zoë Valdés, *La nada cotidiana* (Barcelona: Emecé Editores, 1995), 15, translation mine; hereafter cited in the text as *La nada.*

14. Miguel Barnet, "Miosvatis," trans. Chris Brandt, *The New Yorker,* 26 January 1998, 70–74, 71; hereafter cited in the text.

Conclusion

1. Guillermo Cabrera Infante, *Mea Cuba,* trans. Kenneth Hall (New York: Farrar, Straus Giroux, 1994), 14.

2. José David Saldívar, *The Dialectics of Our America: Genealogy, Cultural Critique, and Literary History* (Durham, N.C.: Duke University Press, 1991), 5; hereafter cited in the text.

3. Alberto Moreiras, "Afterword: Pastiche Identity, and Allegory of Allegory," in *Latin American Identity and Constructions of Difference,* ed. Amaryll Chanady (Minneapolis: University of Minnesota Press, 1994), 204–238, 234.

4. Dolores Prida and Miguel Algarín, PEN American Center Latino Literature Festival, panel discussion, "How Has Latino Writing Evolved over the Past Twenty Years?" New York, 24 May 1996.

Selected Bibliography

PRIMARY WORKS

Alvarez, Julia. *How the García Girls Lost Their Accents.* New York: Plume, 1992.
———. *In the Time of the Butterflies.* New York: Plume, 1994.
———. "Grounds for Fiction," lecture, New York Public Library, 18 February 1997.
———. *¡Yo!* Chapel Hill: Algonquin Books, 1997.
Arenas, Reinaldo. *Celestino antes del alba.* Buenos Aires: Editorial Brújula, 1968.
———. *El mundo alucinante.* Mexico: Editorial Diógenes, 1973.
———. *Termina el desfile.* Barcelona: Seis Barral. 1981.
———. *Cantando en el pozo.* Barcelona: Argos Vergara, 1982.
———. *Otra vez el mar.* Barcelona: Argos Vergara, 1982.
———. *El palacio de las blanquísimas mofetas.* Barcelona: Argos Vergara, 1983.
———. *Arturo, la estrella más brillante.* Barcelona: Montesinos, 1984.
———. *Farewell to the Sea: A Novel of Cuba.* Trans. Andrew Hurley. New York: Avon, 1987.
———. *The Ill-Fated Peregrinations of Fray Servando.* Trans. Andrew Hurley. New York: Avon, 1987.
———. *La loma del ángel.* Malaga: Dador/ediciones, 1987.
———. *The Palace of the White Skunks.* Trans. Andrew Hurley. New York: Avon, 1987.
———. *Singing from the Well.* Trans. Andrew Hurley. New York: Viking, 1987.
———. *El portero.* Malaga: Dador/ediciones, 1989.
———. *Viaje a la Habana: Novela en tres viajes.* Madrid: Mondadori, 1990.
———. *El asalto.* Miami: Ediciones Universal, 1991.
———. *The Doorman.* Trans. Dolores M. Koch. New York: Grove Weidenfeld, 1991.
———. *El color del verano.* Miami: Ediciones Universal, 1991.
———. *Antes que anochezca: Autobiografía.* Barcelona: Tusquets, 1992.
———. *Before Night Falls.* Trans. Dolores M. Koch. New York: Viking, 1993.
———. *The Assault.* Trans. Andrew Hurley. New York: Viking, 1994.
———. *Adiós a mamá: De la Habana a Nueva York.* Barcelona: Altera, 1995.
Barnet, Miguel. *La canción de Rachel.* Barcelona: Editorial Estela, 1970.
———. *Akeke y la jutía: Fábulas cubanas.* Havana: UNEAC, 1978.
———. *Gallego.* Havana: Editorial Letras Cubanas, 1983.
———. *La vida real.* Madrid: Ediciones Alfaguara, 1984.
———. *Oficio de angel.* Madrid: Alfaguara, 1989.

———. *Rachel's Song.* Trans. W. Nick Hill. Willamantic, Conn.: Curbstone Press, 1991.

———. "Miosvatis." Trans. Chris Brandt. *The New Yorker,* 26 January 1998, 70–74.

Cabrera Infante, Guillermo. *Vista del amanecer en el trópico.* Barcelona: Seix Barral, 1974.

———. *La Habana para un infante difunto.* Barcelona: Seix Barral, 1980.

———. *View of Dawn in the Tropics.* London: Faber and Faber, 1988.

———. *Three Trapped Tigers.* Trans. David Gardner and Suzanne Jill Levine, with the author. London: Faber and Faber, 1990.

———. *Tres tristes tigres.* Caracas: Biblioteca Ayacucho, 1990.

———. *Mea Cuba.* Barcelona: Plaza and Janés Editores/Cambio 16, 1992.

———. *Mea Cuba.* Trans. Kenneth Hall, with the author. New York: Farrar Straus Giroux, 1994.

———. *Delito por bailar el chachachá.* Madrid: Santillana, 1995.

———. *Arcadia todas las noches.* Madrid: Alfaguara, 1996.

Carpentier, Alejo. *Explosion in a Cathedral.* Trans. John Sturrock. Boston: Little, Brown, 1963.

———. *El acoso.* Havana: Instituto del Libro, 1969.

———. *The War of Time.* Trans. Frances Partridge. London: Gollancz, 1970.

———. *¡Écue-Yamba-Ó!: Novela afrocubana.* Montevideo: Sandino, 1973.

———. *Guerra del tiempo.* Buenos Aires: Ediciones Corregidor, 1973.

———. *El recurso del método.* Madrid: Siglo Veintiuno Editores, 1974.

———. *Derecho de asilo.* Havana: Editorial Arte y Literatura, 1976.

———. *Reasons of State.* Trans. Frances Partridge. New York: Knopf, 1976.

———. *El reino de este mundo.* Buenos Aires: Editorial Quetzal, 1977.

———. *El arpa y la sombra.* Mexico: Siglo Veintiuno Editores, 1979.

———. *Concierto barroco: Novela.* Mexico: Siglo Veintiuno, 1979.

———. *La consagración de la primavera: Novela.* Mexico: Siglo Veintiuno, 1979.

———. *Los pasos perdidos.* Ed. Roberato González Echevarría. Madrid: Cátedra, 1985.

———. *Concierto Barroco.* Trans. Asa Zatz. Tulsa, Okla.: Council Oak Books, 1988.

———. *The Chase.* Trans. Alfred Mac Adam. New York: Farrar, Straus and Giroux, 1989.

———. *The Lost Steps.* Trans. Harriet de Onís. New York: Noonday Press, 1989.

———. *El siglo de las luces.* Ed. Ambrosio Fornet. Madrid: Ediciones Cátedra, 1989.

———. *The Harp and the Shadow.* Trans. Thomas Christensen and Carol Christensen. San Francisco: Mercury House, 1990.

———. Prologue to *The Kingdom of This World.* Trans. Alfred MacAdam. *Review: Latin American Literature and the Arts* 47 (Fall 1993): 29–31.

———. *The Kingdom of This World.* Trans. Harriet de Onís. New York: Noonday Press, 1994.

Cirules, Enrique. *Los perseguidos.* Havana: Editorial Arte y Literatura, 1971.

———. *El corredor de caballos.* Havana: Letras Cubanas, 1980.

———. *Conversación con el último norteamericano.* Havana: Editorial Letras Cubanas, 1988.

———. *Extraña lluvia en la tormenta.* Havana: UNEAC, 1988.

Cisneros, Sandra. *The House on Mango Street.* Houston: Arte Público, 1988.

———. *Woman Hollering Creek, and Other Stories.* New York: Random House, 1991.

Desnoes, Edmundo. *No hay problema.* Havana: Ediciones R, 1961.

———. *El cataclismo.* Havana: Ediciones R, 1965.

———. *Inconsolable Memories,* translated by the author. New York: New American Library, 1967.

———. *Memorias del subdesarrollo.* Mexico: Joaquín Moritz, 1983.

———, ed. *Los dispositivos en la flor: Cuba, literatura desde la revolución.* Hanover: Ediciones del Norte, 1981.

Díaz, Jesús. *Los años duros.* Havana: Editorial Letras Cubanas, 1981.

———. *Las iniciales de la tierra.* Havana: Letras Cubanas, 1987.

———. *La piel y la máscara.* Barcelona: Editorial Anagrama, 1996.

Didion, Joan. *Miami.* New York: Simon and Schuster, 1987.

Fernández, Pablo Armando. *Los niños se despiden.* Buenos Aires: Centro Editor de América Latina, 1971.

———. *Otro golpe de dados.* Madrid: S.S.A.G., 1993.

Fernández, Roberto G. *Cuentos sin rumbo.* Miami: Ediciones Universal, 1975.

———. *La vida es un special, .75.* Miami: Ediciones Universal, 1981.

———. *La montaña rusa.* Houston: Arte Público, 1985.

———. *Raining Backwards.* Houston: Arte Público, 1988.

———. *Holy Radishes!* Houston: Arte Público, 1995.

Fornet, Ambrosio, ed. *Antología del cuento cubano contemporáneo.* Mexico: Ediciones Era, 1967.

———, ed. *Cuentos de la revolución cubana.* Santiago, Chile: Editorial Universitaria, 1971.

García, Cristina. *Dreaming in Cuban.* New York: Ballantine Books, 1993.

———. *The Agüero Sisters.* New York: Knopf, 1997.

Girona, Julio. *Seis horas y más.* Havana: Editorial Letras Cubanas, 1990.

Gómez Peña, Guillermo. "Border Brujo: A Performance Poem." *TDR: The Drama Review* 35, no. 3 (1991): 48–66.

———. *Warrior for Gringostroika: Essays, Performance Texts, and Poetry.* St. Paul: Graywolf Press, 1993.

———. *The New World Border: Prophecies, Poems, and Loqueras for the End of the Century.* San Francisco: City Lights, 1996.

Hijuelos, Oscar. *The Mambo Kings Play Songs of Love.* New York: Perennial Library, 1990.

———. *The Fourteen Sisters of Emilio Montez O'Brien.* New York: Farrar, Straus and Giroux, 1993.

————. *Our House in the Last World*. New York: Persea Books, 1993.

————. *Mr. Ives' Christmas*. New York: HarperCollins, 1995.

————. *Empress of the Splendid Season*. New York: HarperFlamingo, 1999.

Hinojosa, Rolando. *Klail City y sus alrededores*. Havana: Casa de las Américas, 1976.

————. *Mi Querido Rafa*. Houston: Arte Público, 1981.

————. *Rites and Witness: A Comedy*. Houston: Arte Público, 1982.

————. *Dear Rafe*. Houston: Arte Público, 1985.

————. *Partners in Crime: A Rafe Buenrostro Mystery*. Houston: Arte Público, 1985.

————. *Claros varones de Belken/Fair Gentlemen of Belken County*. Trans. Julia Cruz. Tempe, Ariz.: Bilingual Press, 1986.

————. *Klail City: A Novel*. Houston: Arte Público, 1987.

————. *Becky and Her Friends*. Houston: Arte Público, 1990.

————. *Los amigos de Becky*. Houston: Arte Público, 1991.

————. *The Useless Servants*. Houston: Arte Público, 1993.

————. *Estampas del valle*. Tempe: Editorial Bilingüe, 1994.

Lezama Lima, José. *La expresión americana*. Santiago de Chile: Editorial Universitaria, 1969.

————. *Las eras imaginarias*. Madrid: Editorial Fundamentos, 1971.

————. *Paradiso*. Trans. Gregory Rabassa. London: Secker and Warburg, 1974.

————. *Confluencias: Selección de ensayos*. Ed. Abel E. Prieto. Havana: Letras Cubanas, 1988.

————. *Paradiso*. Edición Crítica. Ed. Cintio Vitier. Buenos Aires: Colección Archivos, 1988.

————. *Oppiano Licario*. Madrid: Cátedra, 1989.

————. *Cuentos*. Ed. Virgilio López Lemus. Quito: Libresa, 1994.

————. *Juego de las decapitaciones*. Barcelona: Montesinos Editor, 1994.

Martínez, Demetria. *MotherTongue*. Tempe, Ariz.: Bilingual Press/Editorial Bilingüe, 1994.

Méndez Capote, Renée. *Memorias de una cubanita que nació con el siglo*. Havana: Bolsilibros Unión, 1964.

Montejo, Esteban. *Biografía de un cimarrón*. Ed. Miguel Barnet. Barcelona: Ediciones Ariel, 1968.

————. *Autobiography of a Runaway Slave*. Trans. W. Nick Hill. Willamantic, Conn.: Curbstone, 1994.

Obejas, Achy. *We Came All the Way from Cuba So You Could Dress like This?* Pittsburgh: Cleis Press, 1994.

————. *Memory Mambo*. Pittsburgh: Cleis Press, 1996.

Ortiz, Fernando. *Contrapunteo cubano del tabaco y el azúcar*. Barcelona: Editorial Ariel, 1973.

————. *Cuban Counterpoint: Tobacco and Sugar*. Trans. Harriet de Onís. Durham, N.C.: Duke University Press, 1995.

Perera, Victor. *Rites, a Guatemalan Boyhood.* San Diego: Harcourt Brace Jovanovich, 1986.

———. *Unfinished Conquest: The Guatemalan Tragedy.* Berkeley: University of California Press, 1993.

Poey, Delia, and Virgil Suárez, eds. *Little Havana Blues: A Cuban-American Literature Anthology.* Houston: Arte Público, 1996.

Rieff, David. *The Exile: Cuba in the Heart of Miami.* New York: Simon and Schuster, 1993.

Santiago, Esmeralda. *When I Was Puerto Rican.* Reading: Addison-Wesley, 1993.

———. *América's Dream.* New York: HarperCollins, 1996.

Sayles, John. *Los Gusanos.* New York: HarperCollins, 1991.

Suárez, Virgil. *The Cutter.* New York: Ballantine, 1991.

———. "Settlements." In *Iguana Dreams: New Latino Fiction,* ed. Delia Poey and Virgil Suárez, 297–320. New York: HarperPerennial, 1992.

———. *Welcome to the Oasis and Other Stories.* Houston: Arte Público, 1992.

———. *Havana Thursdays.* Houston: Arte Público, 1995.

———. *Going Under.* Houston: Arte Público, 1996.

Taibo, Paco Ignacio, II. *Cosa fácil.* Barcelona: Editorial Grijalbo, 1977.

———. *Héroes convocados.* Mexico: Editorial Grijalbo, 1982.

———. *Algunas nubes.* Mexico: Leega Literaria, 1985.

———. *Sombra de la sombra.* Mexico: Planeta, 1986.

———. *No habrá final feliz.* Mexico: Planeta, 1989.

———. *Regreso a la misma ciudad y bajo la lluvia.* Mexico: Planeta, 1989.

———. *Amorosos fantasmas.* Mexico: Promexa, 1990.

———. *Calling All Heroes.* Trans. John Mitchell and Ruth Mitchell de Agular. Kaneohe, Hawaii: Plover Press, 1990.

———. *Cuatro manos.* Managua: Editorial Vanguardia, 1990.

———. *An Easy Thing.* Trans. William I. Neuman. New York: Viking, 1990.

———. *Four Hands.* Trans. Laura C. Dail. New York: St. Martin's Press, 1990.

———. *Sueños de frontera.* Mexico: Promexa, 1990.

———. *Desvanecidos difuntos.* Mexico: Promexa, 1991.

———. *The Shadow of the Shadow.* Trans. William I. Neuman. New York: Viking, 1991.

———. *Doña Eustolia blandió el cuchillo cebollero y otras historias.* Mexico: Joaquín Moritz, 1992.

———. *Some Clouds.* Trans. William I. Neuman. New York: Viking, 1992.

———. *Adiós, Madrid.* Mexico: Promexa, 1993.

———. *La bicicleta de Leonardo.* Mexico: Joaquín Moritz, 1993.

———. *No Happy Ending.* Trans. William I. Neuman. New York: Mysterious Press, 1993.

———. *Life Itself.* Trans. Beth Hanson. New York: Mysterious Press, 1994.

———. *Nomás los muertos están bien contentos.* Mexico: Joaquín Moritz, 1994.

———. *Leonardo's Bicycle.* Trans. Martin Michael Roberts. New York: Mysterious Press, 1995.

————. *La vida misma.* Tafalla: Txalaparta, 1995.

————. *De paso.* Barcelona: Virus, 1996.

————. *Return to the Same City.* New York: Mysterious Press, 1996.

————. *Insurgencia mi amor.* Mexico: El Atajo, 1997.

————. *Sintiendo que el campo de batalla.* Tafalla: Txalaparta, 1997.

Valdés, Zoë. *Sangre azul.* Havana: Letras Cubanas, 1994.

————. *La hija del embajador.* Baleares: Bitzoc, 1995.

————. *La nada cotidiana.* Barcelona: Emecé Editores, 1995.

————. *Cólera de ángeles.* Barcelona: Textuel, 1996.

————. *Te di la vida entera.* Barcelona: Planeta, 1996.

————. *Café nostalgia.* Barcelona: Planeta, 1997.

————. *Yocandra in the Paradise of Nada: A Novel of Cuba.* Trans. Sabina Cienfuegos. New York: Arcade Publishers, 1997.

Veiga, Marisella. "Fresh Fruit." In *Iguana Dreams: New Latino Fiction,* ed. Delia Poey and Virgil Suárez, 351–53. New York: HarperPerennial, 1992.

Yglesias, Rafael. *Dr. Neruda's Cure for Evil.* New York: Warner Books, 1996.

SECONDARY WORKS

Agüero, Luis. "La novela." *Casa de las Américas* 4, nos. 22–23 (January–April 1964): 60–67.

Alvarez, Julia. "Conversation with Julia Alvarez." Interview by Heather Rosario-Sievert. *Review: Latin American Literature and the Arts* 54 (Spring 1997): 31–37.

Arias, Salvador, ed. *Recopilación de textos sobre Alejo Carpentier.* Havana: Casa de las Américas, 1977.

Barnet, Miguel. *La fuente viva.* Havana: Letras Cubanas, 1983.

————. *Autógrafos cubanos.* Havana: Ediciones Unión, 1990.

Benedetti, Mario, Alejo Carpentier, Julio Cortázar, and Miguel Barnet. *Literatura y arte nuevo en Cuba.* Barcelona: Editorial Estela, 1971.

Benítez Rojo, Antonio. *La isla que se repite.* Hanover: Ediciones del Norte, 1982.

————. *The Repeating Island: The Caribbean and the Postmodern Perspective.* Trans. James Maraniss. Durham, N.C.: Duke University Press, 1992.

Blanco Aguinaga, Carlos. *De mitólogos y novelistas.* Madrid: Ediciones Turner, 1975.

Bueno, Salvador. *Medio Siglo de literatura cubana.* Havana: Comisión de la Unesco, 1953.

————. *Historia de la literatura cubana.* Havana: Ministerio de Educación, 1963.

Chanady, Amaryll, ed. *Latin American Identity and Constructions of Difference.* Minneapolis: University of Minnesota Press, 1994.

Cortázar, Julio. "Para llegar a Lezama Lima." *Union* 5, no. 4 (October–December 1966): 36–60.

Falquez-Certain, Miguel, ed. *New Voices in Latin American Literature.* Jackson Heights: Ollantay Center for the Arts, 1993.

Fernández Retamar, Roberto. *Calibán y otros ensayos.* Havana: Editorial Arte y Literatura, 1979.

———. *Caliban and Other Essays.* Trans. Edward Baker. Minneapolis: University of Minnesota Press, 1989.

Fernández Guerra, Angel. "Cimarrón y Rachel: Un continuum." In *Nuevos críticos cubanos,* ed. José Prats Sariol, 528–37. Havana: Letras Cubanas, 1983.

Figueredo, Danilo H. "The Evolution of Cuban-American Literature." *Multicultural Review,* March 1997, 18–28.

Fornet, Ambrosio. *En tres y dos: Problemas de la crítica literaria en Cuba.* Havana: Ediciones R, 1964.

———. *En blanco y negro.* Havana: Editorial Arte y Literatura, 1979.

———, ed. *Cine, literatura, y sociedad.* Havana: Letras Cubanas, 1982.

Foster, David William. *Cuban Literature: A Research Guide.* New York: Garland, 1985.

Gikandi, Simon. *Writing in Limbo: Modernism and Caribbean Literature.* Ithaca, N.Y.: Cornell University Press, 1992.

Gil, Lourdes. "La pregunta del forastero: ¿Existe una literatura cubana en Nueva York?" *Brújula/Compass,* nos. 7–8 (Winter 1990): 18–19.

Glissant, Édouard. *Caribbean Discourse: Selected Essays.* Trans. J. Michael Dash. Charlottesville: University Press of Virginia, 1989.

Gutiérrez, Ramón, and Genaro Padilla, eds. *Recovering the U.S. Hispanic Literary Heritage.* Houston: Arte Público, 1993.

Hanchard, Michael. "Intellectual Pursuit." *The Nation,* 19 February 1996, 22–24.

Hernández Lima, Dinorah. *Versiones y re-versiones históricas en la obra de Cabrera Infante.* Madrid: Editorial Pliegos, 1990.

Lago, Eduardo. "De un lado el Sultán, de otro la narradora: Conversación con Julia Alvarez." *Brújula/Compass* (February 1992): 16–18.

Larsen, Neil. *Reading North by South: On Latin American Literature, Culture, and Politics.* Minneapolis: University of Minnesota Press, 1995.

López, Iraida H. "Dreaming in Cuban: An Interview with Cristina García." *Brújula/Compass,* no. 16 (Spring 1993): 15–17.

Luis, William, ed. *Voices from Under: Black Narrative in Latin America and the Caribbean.* Westport, Conn.: Greenwood Press, 1984.

———. *Literary Bondage: Slavery in Cuban Narrative.* Austin: University of Texas Press, 1990.

Maratos, Daniel C., and Marnesba D. Hill. *Cuban Exile Writers: A Bibliographic Handbook.* Metuchen: Scarecrow Press, 1986.

Pérez Firmat, Gustavo. *The Cuban Condition: Translation and Identity in Modern Cuban Literature.* New York: Cambridge University Press, 1989.

———. *Do the Americas Have a Common Literature?* Durham, N.C.: Duke University Press, 1990.

————. *Life on the Hyphen: The Cuban-American Way.* Austin: University of Texas Press, 1994.

————. *Next Year in Cuba: A Cubano's Coming-of-Age in America.* New York: Anchor Books, 1995.

Portuondo, José Antonio. *Bosquejo histórico de las letras cubanas.* Havana: Editorial Nacional de Cuba, 1962.

————. *Itinerario estético de la Revolución Cubana.* Havana: Letras Cubanas, 1979.

————. *Capítulos de la literatura cubana.* Havana: Letras Cubanas, 1981.

Prats Sariol, José. *Criticar al crítico.* Havana: UNEAC, 1983.

————, ed. *Nuevos críticos cubanos.* Havana: Editorial Letras Cubanas, 1983.

Prida, Dolores, and Miguel Algarín. PEN American Center Latino Literature Festival. Panel discussion, "How Has Latino Writing Evolved over the Past Twenty Years?" New York, 24 May 1996.

Rama, Angel. *La novela en América Latina: Panoramas, 1920–1980.* Bogotá: Instituto Colombiano de Cultura, 1982.

————. *Transculturación narrativa en América Latina.* Mexico: Fundación Angel Rama, 1982.

Richardson, Michael, ed. *Refusal of the Shadow: Surrealism and the Caribbean.* Trans. Krysztof Fijalkowski and Michael Richardson. London: Verso, 1996.

Rodríguez Feo, José. *Mi correspondencia con Lezama Lima.* Havana: UNEAC, 1989.

Rumbaut, Rubén. "The Post-exile Generation." *Cuban Affairs* 3 (Summer–Fall 1996): 4–6.

Said, Edward. *The World, the Text, and the Critic.* Cambridge: Harvard University Press, 1983.

————. *Culture and Imperialism.* New York: Vintage, 1994.

————. "Speaking Truth to Power: The Public Intellectual at the End of the Twentieth Century." Roundtable discussion with Edward Said, Susan Sontag, and Juan Goytisolo, New York University, 18 April 1997.

Saldívar, José David. *The Dialectics of Our America: Genealogy, Cultural Critique, and Literary History.* Durham, N.C.: Duke University Press, 1991.

Semprun, Jorge. *Literature or Life.* Trans. Linda Coverdale. New York: Viking, 1997.

Simón, Pedro, ed. *Recopilación de textos sobre José Lezama Lima.* Havana: Casa de las Américas, 1970.

Smorkaloff, Pamela Maria. *Readers and Writers in Cuba: A Social History of Print Culture, 1830s–1990s.* New York: Garland, 1997.

Souza, Raymond D. *Major Cuban Novelists: Innovation and Tradition.* Columbia: University of Missouri Press, 1976.

————. *The Poetic Fiction of José Lezama Lima.* Columbia: University of Missouri Press, 1983.

————. *Guillermo Cabrera Infante: Two Islands, Many Worlds.* Austin: University of Texas Press, 1996.

Weiss, Rachel, and Alan West. *Being América: Essays on Art, Literature, and Identity from Latin America.* Fredonia, N.Y.: White Pine Press, 1991.

Index

acoso, El, 14–15
Adam, the Latin American writer as, 10–11, 13, 34
Afro-Cubans, 28
Age of Enlightenment, the, 15, 25
Algarín, Miguel, 81
alienation, as literary theme, 11, 12, 16, 24, 49–50, 71
Alvarez, Julia, 8, 62–64, 65, 66, 70; *How the García Girls Lost Their Accents*, 8, 67–68, 70; *In the Time of the Butterflies*, 62–63; *¡Yo!*, 68
Amazon, the, 13, 14
American aesthetic, fin de siècle, 78
American Dream, the, 37, 48
areitos, 53
Arenas, Reinaldo, 9, 19, 25; *El mundo alucinante* 19, 25
Autobiography of a Runaway Slave (Biografía de un cimarrón), 19, 27, 28, 30, 31

Barnet, Miguel, 6, 9, 28, 30, 31, 72, 76; "Miosvatis," 72–73
baroque, the, in Latin American and Caribbean literature, 13, 16, 17, 18, 19, 20, 68
Batista, Fulgencio, 21, 37
Baudelaire, Charles Pierre, 28
Benítez Rojo, Antonio, 33; *The Repeating Island*, 33
bilingualism and biculturalism in Latino and Latin American literature, 70
Borrero, Esteban and Juana, 7
Brathwaite, Kamau, 64

Cabrera Infante, Guillermo, 76; *Mea Cuba*, 76, 77
Caliban, in Shakespeare's *The Tempest*, 60
Caribbean, pre-Columbian history of the, 53
Caribbean novel, the, 33
Carpentier, Alejo, 2, 3, 5–6, 8, 9, 10, 11, 13–16, 18, 20, 29, 31, 32, 34, 61, 66, 67; "contexts" as literary practice,

12; theory of the novel in Latin America, 12
Carrión, Miguel de, 2
Casa José Lezama Lima, the, 16
Casas, Bartolomé de las, 39
Chanady, Amaryll, ed., *Latin American Identity and Constructions of Difference*, 80
Chiampi, Irlemar, 30
civilization vs. barbarism debate, 26
Cold War, the, 7, 61, 75
Consagración de la primavera, 6, 13
contemporary Cuban literature, strains in, 5
Creole aristocracy, nineteenth century, 3
Cuban-American identity, 2, 16, 32, 34, 67; Pérez Firmat on, 44, 47; social construction of, 27–28; in Virgil Suárez, 49–50
Cuban-American monolith, the, 36
Cuban-American narrative, 2, 16, 27, 31, 36, 44, 67, 82
Cuban bourgeoisie, the, 21, 22, 23, 33; social construction of whiteness by the, 39
Cuban canon, twentieth-century, 9, 16, 31; diaspora writers and the, 45, 81–82
Cuban diaspora, 7, 9, 80, 81; diaspora writers, 77–78
Cuban identity, 2, 16, 28, 29, 67; as *dream* in Cristina García, 45–46; as *dream* in Roberto G. Fernández, 55; nationalism and, 33
Cuban novel, the, 10, 33, 81
Cuban Republic, the, 21, 22, 28, 29, 33, 76

dependency theorists, Latin American, 60
Desnoes, Edmundo, 6, 9, 19, 21, 22, 23, 71; *Los dispositivos en la flor*, 6
Díaz, Jesús, 2
Didion, Joan, *Miami*, 80
discovery of America, the, 16

Éécue-Yamba-Ó!, 29–30
1898, 2
emigration and absence as themes in contemporary Cuban fiction, 72
European Romantics, the, 12; quest for freedom, 12
exile, 4, 7, 70; as theme in *El mundo alucinante*, 26; in *Memory Mambo*, 34; in Virgil Suárez, 49; in Edward Said, 64
existentialism, 23, 24
Explosion in a Cathedral (El siglo de las luces), 6, 8, 13, 14, 15, 16

Faulkner, William, 61, 66
Fernández, Pablo Armando, 9, 19, 21; *Los niños se despiden*, 19; significance of language in, 20
Fernández, Roberto G., 51; bilingualism in the novels of, 55–56; *La vida es un special*, .75, 51–56
Fernández Guerra, Angel, 28
Fernández Retamar, Roberto, 60, 61; *Caliban and Other Essays (Calibán y otros ensayos)*, 60–61
French revolution, the, 13, 15, 16
Fuentes, Carlos, 23; *Cristóbal Nonato*, 69
García, Cristina, 45; *Dreaming in Cuban*, 45–46
García Márquez, Gabriel, 33, 61, 66
gay themes in contemporary Cuban literature, 79
Girona, Julio, 76, 77; *Seis horas y más*, 77
Glissant, Édouard, 36
golden age, the, 10
Gómez Peña, Guillermo, 65
González, Reynaldo, 17
Gutiérrez, Ramón, 1

Haitian revolution, 5, 13
Hamlet, 12
Hanchard, Michael, 66; contemporary African-American intellectuals and Latin American thought, 66
Harp and the Shadow, The (El arpa y la sombra), 14, 16
Hemingway, Ernest, 23
Heredia, José María de, 25

here/there axis and novelistic structure in Carpentier, 13, 67
Hijuelos, Oscar, 44, 46, 50; *Mr. Ive's Christmas*, 44; *Our House in the Last World*, 44, 46, 50
Hinojosa, Rolando, 65; *Klail City y sus alrededores*, 66; *Partners in Crime*, 66
Hiroshima, mon amour, 23
historiography, 27; and the novel, 31
history as spiral, concept in Carpentier, 13, 15, 18
Hughes, Victor, 14, 15, 16
hyphenated writers, 7, 67, 78

Inconsolable Memories (Memorias del subdesarrollo), 19, 21, 22, 30, 71; theme of underdevelopment in, 22
independence movements in Latin America, 25
independence wars, Cuba, 22, 28
intergenerational conflict, 3, 5, 52

Jesús, Pedro de, and the Cuban gay short story, 79
journey as literary theme, 3, 8, 10, 18, 20, 25, 32, 33, 50–51
"Journey Back to the Source," 3, 14
Joyce, James, 17

Kingdom of This World, The (El reino de este mundo), 5, 13
Kozer, José, 44
labor migration, 61

Lao-tzu, 23
Larsen, Neil, 27
Latin American artist, the, 11; problematic of, 11
Latin American culture, theory of, 6, 10
Latin American literary "boom," the, 61
Latin American novel, the contemporary, 12
Latino literature, 61; relationship to Latin American literature and Cuban-American narratives, 64–65
Laurel, Stan, 63, 68
Lezama Lima, José, 8, 9, 16, 17, 19, 20, 22, 32; *Paradiso*, 8, 16, 17, 18, 19, 22

liberation, as literary theme, 16, 25
literacy campaign, 21
Little War of 1912, the, 28
Lost Steps, The (Los pasos perdidos), 6, 10, 11, 12, 13, 14, 15, 61
Luis, William, 31
Lukàcs, György, 70; *The Theory of the Novel*, 70

Machado, Gerardo, 7, 29
Mariel émigrés, 47
maroons, 28, 31
Marshalle, Paule, 64
Martí, José, 7, 63, 77; "Nuestra América" as cultural manifesto, 60–61
Martínez, Demetria, 70; *MotherTongue*, 70; bilingualism in, 70
Melville, Herman, 66
Memorias de una cubanita que nació con el siglo, 19, 21–22, 30, 76; as catharsis, 21; consumption in, 21
memory as literary theme, 3, 4, 8, 10, 27, 30–31, 32, 35
Méndez Capote, Renée, 9, 19, 21, 22, 31, 33, 76
Miami enclave, the, 53, 56
Mier, Fray Servando Teresa de, 25
Missile Crisis of 1962, the, 24
Montaigne, Michel de, 23
Montejo, Esteban, 28, 29, 31
Moreira, Alberto, 80
Morrison, Toni, 66

Neruda, Pablo, 23
nihilism, 23
1960s, the, 19, 23; Cuban novels of, 20; in Cuba and Latin America, 25, 26, 27
novela-testimonio, la (*see also* testimonial novel), 19, 26, 27, 30, 76

Obejas, Achy, 2, 3, 9, 31, 46, 64–66; *Memory Mambo*, 31, 32–43, 48, 82; "We Came All the Way from Cuba So You Could Dress like This?," 3, 4, 31
October revolution, the, 13, 15, 16
Orígenes journal, the, 16; Orígenes group, 17

Orinoco river, in *The Lost Steps*, 13
Ortiz, Fernando, 7; *Cuban Counterpoint*, 7

Padilla, Genaro, 1
Perera, Victor, 62; "The New Indian versus the New Maya," *Unfinished Conquest*, 62
Pérez Firmat, Gustavo, 44–45, 46, 56, 80; *Life on the Hyphen*, 44, 56, 80
positivism, 39
Prida, Dolores, 81

quest for liberation, the, as literary theme, 25
Quiroga, Horacio, 56

Rachel's Song (La canción de Rachel), 19, 28, 29
real maravilloso, lo, theory of, 5, 6, 13; (*see also* the marvellous real, 13, 14, 30, 32, 68)
revolution of 1959, 2; novels that deal with, 2, 6–7, 13, 21, 23, 36, 45, 71; and the writing of Lezama Lima's *Paradiso*, 17
Rieff, David, 80; *Exile: Cuba in the Heart of Miami*, 80
Rodríguez Feo, José, 17
Rodríguez de Tío, Lola, 22
rural peasantry, 28

Said, Edward, 63, 64, 65, 70; *Culture and Imperialism*, 63–64, 70
Saldívar, José David, 62; *The Dialectics of Our America*, 62
Santiago, Esmeralda, 70; *When I Was Puerto Rican*, 70
Sayles, John, 65, *Los gusanos*, 65
Semprun, Jorge, 67; *Literature or Life*, 67
slave barracks, social life in, 28, 31
Souza, Raymond, 10, 17, 18
Spanish civil war, the, 13
Stendahl, 23
Suárez, Virgil, 46; ennui, as theme in, 47; *Going Under*, 48–51; "Settlements," 47–48; "Welcome to the Oasis," 47; *Welcome to the Oasis and Other Stories*, 47

surrealism, 5
syncretism , New World, 13; and transculturation, 70

Taibo, Paco Ignacio, 63, 64, 70; *Four Hands*, 63, 68–69
Tientos y diferencias: Problemática actual de la novela latinoamericana, 12

Valdés, Zoë, 70; *La nada cotidiana*, 70–72
Veiga, Marisella, 56; "Fresh Fruit," 56–59

Vian, Boris, 71; *L'écume des jours*, 71
vida real, La, 30
Villa, Pancho, 63, 68
Villaverde, Cirilo, 7; *Cecilia Valdés*, 77

Western civilization, 11; in Carpentier, 11–12

Ybor City, 44
Yglesias, Rafael, 43; *Dr. Neruda's Cure for Evil*, 43–44

The Author

Pamela Maria Smorkaloff is a Cuban-American scholar who has taught in the graduate program in Latin American and Caribbean Studies at New York University for the last 10 years and is currently on the faculty of Montclair State University. She is the author of a study of Cuban literary history, *Readers and Writers in Cuba: A Social History of Print Culture, 1830s–1990s* (Garland, Latin American Studies, 1997); *If I Could Write This in Fire: An Anthology of Literature from the Caribbean* (edited) (The New Press, 1994), and numerous articles on Latin American and Caribbean literature and cultural history. She holds a doctorate in Latin American literature from New York University.

The Editor

David William Foster is Regents' Professor of Spanish and director of Spanish graduate studies at Arizona State University, where he also chairs the publications committee of the Center for Latin American Studies. He is known for his extensive contributions in the field of Latin American literary bibliography and reference works. In addition, he has published numerous monographs on Latin American literature, with emphasis on theater and narrative, the most recent of which is *Violence in Argentine Literature: Cultural Responses to Tyranny* (University of Missouri Press, 1995).